C000264367

35 Checklists for Human Resource Development

35 Checklists for Human Resource Development

Ian MacKay

Gower

in association with

the Institute of Training and Development

© Ian MacKay, 1989

All rights reserved. No part of this publication may be reproduced, stored in a retrieval system, or transmitted in any form or by any means, electronic, mechanical, photocopying, recording, or otherwise without the prior permission of Gower Publishing Company Limited.

Published by
Gower Publishing Company Limited
Gower House
Croft Road
Aldershot
Hants GU11 3HR
England

Gower Publishing Company
Old Post Road
Brookfield
Vermont 05036
USA

British Library Cataloguing in Publication Data

MacKay, Ian
    35 checklists for human resource development
    1. Personnel management
    I. Title II. Institute of Training and Development
    658.3

    ISBN 0-566-02823-9

Printed and bound in Great Britain by
Courier International Ltd, Tiptree, Essex

Contents

List of figures

Foreword

by Sir James Munn, OBE FITD
President, Institute of Training and Development

Ian MacKay's checklists have been highly acclaimed by ITD members who have had the advantage of seeing most of them published at regular intervals over the past four years in the ITD journal 'Training and Development'. They have proved to be an excellent aide mémoire for the busy trainer and I am pleased they are now being made available in this collected edition for easy reference.

Preface

Airline pilots must complete a final pre-flight checklist every time they fly. The litany is familiar and the reason is obvious: components and systems may still fail despite previous maintenance. If ignored a malfunction could cause a disaster. Such a checklist ensures that nothing critical is overlooked before departure and is essential to passenger safety. Completion is a standard operating instruction.

In contrast, the checklists shown on the following pages are not standardized. Whilst they can still be used as a maintenance check on systems and skills, their primary aim is to stimulate and focus your thinking, not to provoke simple 'knee-jerk' yes or no responses.

The list of topics is not exclusive, neither is it complete. How you use the checklists and how often you refer to them is obviously your decision. Nevertheless, if reading these pages persuades you that you should address such questions, and many others in the human resourcing and development field, both now and in the future (and perhaps subsequently develop checklists of your own) then they will have succeeded, and, I hope, so will you.

Ian MacKay

Acknowledgements

I would like to acknowledge my debt to colleagues at the Dorset Institute for their help in preparing these checklists. In particular I would like to thank Justus Akinsanya, Frank Davies, Alan Dennett, David Gill and Julia Kiely, with whom six of the lists were written. Bob Anderton, Ron Burns and Mike Jinks also helped in discussing specialist aspects. To David Gill and Julia Kiely I owe a particular debt of gratitude for their unfailing patience and support.

Checklist 20 'Managing your time', which first appeared in Guide to Managing Time (BACIE, 1989) is reproduced by agreement with BACIE.

IM

1 Absenteeism

Non-attendance at work represents a major cause of inefficiency in many organizations. Regular collection, and review, of data on sickness absence, absence resulting from accidents at work, and other absences with and without permission, provide a firm basis for introducing and maintaining counter-measures. An organization's expectations on absenteeism can be emphasized during induction, as can the controls in use and the ultimate corporate response to persistent absenteeism.

Background considerations

1. Do you recognize that absenteeism in your organization is probably a major cause of inefficiency?

2. How big is the problem in your organization?

   - In what way is 'absenteeism' distinguished from 'lateness'?
   - Is the distinction reasonable?
   - By what criteria?

3. Are most employees involved? Or particular groups?

4. Does it occur most amongst:

   - Particular age groups?
   - Full-time or part-time employees?
   - Particular grades of employee (e.g. unskilled, semi-skilled or skilled)?
   - Particular occupations (e.g. process workers)?
   - Particular departments?
   - Married or single employees?
   - Male or female employees?
   - New or longer-service employees?
   - Employees of different ethnic groups?

   Or does it occur after a particular period of service?

Cost

5. Do you know the current cost of absenteeism in your organization? On what basis has the cost been calculated?

6. Have you costed the direct effect of absenteeism on:
   - Production?
   - Scrap/waste levels?
   - Machine down time?
   - Late deliveries?
   - Rescheduling time by management?

   What is the indirect effect on other employees? And on their efficiency?

Measurement and evaluation

7. Is absenteeism measured? How? Are the following formulae used?

Lost time
$$\frac{\text{Number of work hours lost} \times 100}{\text{Total number of possible hours}}$$

Spells of absence
$$\frac{\text{Number of spells of absence in a period}}{\text{Average number employed in the same period}}$$

Number of absences
$$\frac{\text{Number of employees absent once or more in a period}}{\text{Average number employed in the same period}}$$

8. If not, what measures are used? Do they really indicate the extent to which absenteeism is taking place? Are the trends evaluated periodically? If so, how often? Is that often enough?

9. How do the trends compare with those for other organizations in your locality? How do they compare with those for other organizations in your industry? What regional (and national) comparisons can be drawn?

10. If absenteeism is not measured, and trends are not evaluated, what action is indicated? Who should take it? When?
    - Or is it considered that the administrative cost could not be justified? If so, would it be worth re-examining this view now?

Records

11. If absenteeism is measured in your organization, does the absentee records system permit analyses to be made of each employee's attendance and reasons for absence?

12. Does the system analyse reasons for absence by:
    - Sickness (classified by type)?

2

     – Accidents at work?
     – Other absence with permission?
     – Other absence without permission?

13. When was the system set up?

     – Is it periodically examined to establish whether modification/updating is necessary?
     – If not, should it be examined now, not only in terms of what information is recorded, but also how it is recorded?

14. Are you sure that the system provides a sound base on which to analyse the reasons for absenteeism?

     – Are you getting a true picture of the situation and the underlying causes?
       • For instance, to what extent might boredom and frustration with 'uninteresting' work be causing absenteeism? Has the relationship of absentee rates to sick pay arrangements been fully assessed?
       • Further, have individual periods of absenteeism been examined to establish the significance of timing (e.g. does absenteeism 'peak' immediately before resignation)?

15. Who is responsible for administering the system?

16. How long does it take for an absence to be recorded? Is that too long?

Standards

17. Is the organization's expectation on attendance and timekeeping explained at the selection interview? Again during induction?

18. Are the standards the same for *all* employees in the organization, including management? Is a good example set by individual members of management?

     – Is everyone aware of what standards are totally unacceptable to the organization? Are you sure?
       • For instance, what degree of absenteeism would result in a formal warning? Or even in dismissal?

19. Are the absence records of individual employees ever discussed with them?

     – If so, by whom? When? Is a record kept of the discussion in view of possible subsequent disciplinary action (including dismissal)?
     – If not, what should be done?

20. Are all managers and supervisors aware of their personal responsibility for minimizing absenteeism? How do you know?

    – Is it discussed periodically with managers, supervisors and employee representatives?

    – Is it written clearly into every management job description? If not, what action is indicated?

Communication and controls

21.   Who receives information reports on absenteeism? Are they the right people? Are checks made periodically? For example, do *all* supervisors receive copies? How often? Has a check been made recently to evaluate what supervisors actually do about these reports on receiving them?

22.   Who is responsible for:

    – Planning to reduce absenteeism?
    – Taking action to reduce it?
    – Controlling the ongoing effectiveness of the plan?

23.   Are they the right people? Who else should be involved?

    – For example, to what extent is the person responsible for administration (question 15) involved in the above activities? Is a greater involvement indicated?

24.   When was the last time the effectiveness of the plan was reviewed? What was the result of the review? Were specific objectives reformulated and communicated to all concerned?

    – Were these objectives specified strongly enough? Are you sure?
    – What progress has been made in meeting these objectives against the time-scale set?

25.   Is it time the organization's total approach to 'absenteeism' was reviewed again?

    – Who should review it?
    – Who should be consulted?
    – Who should be informed of the results?

How do the answers to these questions compare with those to questions 22 and 23? What further action is indicated?

Development

26.   For instance, is it recognized, by all concerned, that attendance bonuses to reduce absenteeism may never really solve the problem? Would it be worthwhile considering the development of an approach which rewards regular attendance *in kind* (i.e. with time off): in other words, an approach which involves paid leave days which could be left to accrue over a period?

27. When was the last time absenteeism was the subject of a joint consultation meeting? What was the result?

   – Should the topic be included on the agenda for the next meeting? Who should present it?
   – Should it become a regular item on the agenda?

Summary

28. In brief, have the following questions been answered by those responsible for dealing with the effects of absenteeism within the organization?

   – Has the incidence of absenteeism been analysed thoroughly?
   – Has its impact on productivity been examined in detail?
   – Are personal responsibilities clearly identified (particularly those of supervisors)?
   – Do plans exist for improving the situation? Are they proving truly effective?
   – Are these plans revised regularly?

29. What action is indicated *now*?

2 Asking the right questions

Managers spend a large part of their lives at work asking and answering questions, although relatively few are conscious of the various types of questions open to them. Recognizing the different forms that questions can take, and the purposes they serve, may help you to improve your own skill in this respect.

Preliminary diagnosis

1. How often do you ask questions at work? At home? Elsewhere?

2. How many questions, on average, do you estimate you ask each day?

3. To what extent could your performance in asking questions be affecting your job performance overall? Or relationships at home? Or your reputation in other situations?

4. How many hours training in asking questions have you undertaken in the past three years? How many books/articles on the subject have you read in the same period? With what result?

5. How do you rate your skill in asking questions sensitively? During conversations at work? During any interviews you conduct? At meetings? On the telephone? At home? Elsewhere?

   - Are you 'above average'? Or merely 'average'? Or even 'below average'?
   - How do you know?
   - How can you know?

6. On reflection, do you use a wide range of different forms of questions in meeting your various aims? (See Figure 2.1)

   - Are you generally clear about why you are using a particular type of question?
   - What effort do you normally make to 'see' your questions from the

6

other person's point of view?
- Having asked a question, do you invariably allow the person thinking time to produce a measured response?
- How effective are you in encouraging a speaker to continue without saying anything yourself?
- To what extent do you analyse replies to your questions in terms of:
  - What the person seems to be saying?
  - What can be inferred from what is said and how it is said?
  - What is being conveyed by the whole manner of approach to a reply (the non-verbal signals)?
- How often in any sort of conversation do you have a tendency to signal the response you want? Or answer your own questions? Or finish speakers' sentences for them? (See Figure 2.2)
- Just how far do you avoid asking questions which you think may show your ignorance?
- How often do you tend to let your mind wander during a conversation and subsequently mishear people's replies to your questions?
- How often are you asked to repeat your questions?

The future?

7. Do your answers suggest that you could extend your skill in asking questions effectively?

   - What possible action do your answers suggest?
   - What do you believe you should do, if anything? When?

8. What assistance can you seek from colleagues at work? From relatives at home? From others elsewhere? Who will you involve? Who should you involve?

9. Having decided what you will do, and within what time frame, what monitoring is appropriate? In specific terms, how will you measure your progress? When?

Question type	Purpose	Question form	Illustrations
Open	To establish rapport	Contact	Introductory questions/comments to establish the first superficial relationship and to put respondent at ease, e.g. reference to mutually-shared experiences, unusual leisure interests.
	To explore broad background information	General	'Please tell me about . . .?'
	To explore opinions/attitudes	Opinion seeking	'How do you feel about . . .? What do you think about . . .?'
		Trailer	Making a broad comment on a subject and then pausing in anticipation of a response (i.e. the question is hidden)
Probe	To show interest/encouragement	Non-verbal noises	'Ummm?' 'Er?' 'Ah?' 'Oh?' 'Hmmm?' together with appropriate facial expressions (smiles, raised eyebrows) and head movements
		Supportive statements	'I see . . .?' 'And then . . .?' 'That's interesting . . .?' (i.e. tell me more)
		Key word repetition	Repetition of one or two words to encourage further response
		Mirror	Repetition of short reply as a query
	To seek further information	Simple interrogative	'Why?' 'Why not?'
		The pause	Allied to various non-verbal signals

Figure 2.1   Some question forms

8

Question type	Purpose	Question form	Illustrations
		Comparative	'How do your responsibilities now compare with those in your last job?'
		Extension	'How do you mean?' 'Can you tell me more about that?'
		Hypothetical	'What would you do if . . .?' 'How would you feel if . . .?'
	To explore in detail particular opinions/attitudes	Opinion investigation	'Why do you feel that way?' 'Do you have any other reasons for feeling as you do?'
		The reflection	'You think that . . .?' 'It seems to you that . . .?' 'You feel that . . .?'
	To demonstrate understanding/ clarify information already given	Summary	'As I understand it . . .?' 'If I've got it right . . .?' 'So what you're saying is . . .?'
Closed	To establish specific facts/ information	Yes/no response	'Are you . . .?' 'Do you . . .?' 'Have you . . .?'
		Identification of person, time, location, number	'How many people do you have reporting to you?' 'How long did you have that job?'

Figure 2.1 *concluded*

Question type	Purpose	Question form	Illustrations
Counter-product-ive	To prompt desired answer	Leading	'I take it you believe that . . .?' 'You don't *really* think that. . . do you?' 'You must admit that . . .?' 'Isn't it a fact that . . .?'
	To confuse or mislead	Marathon	Asking a question in a rambling, incomprehensible way
		Trick	'Do you drink?'
		Multiple	Two or more questions presented as a package. 'You did say you wouldn't mind being away from home occasionally? Oh and you do have a current driving licence, don't you? I presume it's clean? And, er, by the way . . .?' etc.
		Ambiguous	'What about games?'
	To prevent respondent saying anything	Rhetorical	Answering your own questions: 'Do you . . .?' Of course you do. I always say that . . .?'

Figure 2.2 Question forms to be avoided

3 Assertiveness: First steps

Responding assertively to people and events is one of the criteria for personal success. For most people it is an acquired skill: it can be learned much like any other. To develop your own approach means first taking stock of the ways in which you behave now. The following questions will help you to analyse the beliefs which underpin your behaviour and also provide a springboard for any action you may care to take in becoming more assertive.

1. What sort of person are you? What would be the answers of those who know you?

2. To what extent do you genuinely take responsibility for your own behaviour? For the things you say and do at home, at work and elsewhere? And the ways in which you say them? And do them?

3. Do people have a tendency to hurt or insult you with the things they say about you? And to you?

4. How often do you allow others to make your decisions for you? To manipulate you into making decisions that they want you to make?

5. Just how much do you shift the blame on to others for whatever happens to you?

   - If your answer is 'never', are you sure?
   - Are you ever anxious about the outcome of such events?

6. How satisfied are you with your job currently?

   - Why do you feel this way?
   - What events/people are responsible for your response?

7. What personal development plans have you initiated and followed through in the last six months? In the six months before that?

8. What do your answers to the previous questions say about you?

    - Do they suggest that you are a comparatively submissive or passive sort of person? One who reacts to events? One who denies responsibility? And who expects and allows others to make his or her decisions?
    - If such descriptions are not typical of your behaviour, what descriptions would be more accurate?

9. How far would it be true to say that rather than allowing others to make decisions for you, the reverse applies? That you have a tendency to make others' decisions for them? ('What you should do is obviously to . . .')

10. Do you ever have to put people down? To hurt or insult them with the things you say? If so, how often does this happen?

11. What beliefs about life do you hold? Is one of them that you expect people to live their lives by similar (i.e. your) standards?

12. How often do you interrupt when someone is talking? How often do you change the subject to one you wish to discuss? Just how far do you hear, rather than listen?

13. Are you a perfectionist? Do you expect perfection from others? Do you exclude the possibility of people making mistakes?

    - How often do you over-react when mistakes are made?
    - Do you tend to 'nit-pick'?

14. To what extent could it be said that you block people's progress at work? And deny them job satisfaction?

15. What do your answers to questions 9–14 say about you?

    - Do they suggest that you are a rather aggressive sort of person? One who is particularly decisive on behalf of others? One who does not suffer fools gladly? Who lives by high standards and expects others to do likewise?
    - If such descriptions are no more typical of your behaviour than the descriptions included in questions 3–7, what others would be more accurate?

16. Would people say that you have a tendency to get things done without hurting them or damaging their self esteem? That you are a good listener?

17. Do you tend to make the occasional mistake and, having done so, accept responsibility for the consequences?

18. Do you encourage people to make their own decisions? ('What do you think that you ought to do?')

19. Can you remain cool in your dealings with people, even when provoked?

20. Do you make your own personal decisions? Are you truly independent? Are you sure? Again, do you encourage others to take a similar stance?

21. Are you the sort of person who genuinely helps others to develop themselves? To gain added job satisfaction?

22. What do your answers to questions 16-21 say about you?
    - Do they suggest that you act within your rights as a person? That you are proactive rather than reactive? That you are a realist?
    - That your temper is under firm control? And that you encourage others to act in a similar way?

23. Do your answers to *all* the previous questions tend to indicate that your behaviour approximates more to one particular category as illustrated in Figure 3.1?

Questions 3-7	Questions 9-14	Questions 16-21
Submissive	Aggressive	Assertive

Figure 3.1   Types of behaviour

24. Whatever your response, is it worth probing in more detail into the beliefs surrounding what might be called your 'typical' behaviour, as illustrated in Figure 3.2?

Submissive	Aggressive	Assertive
- people will like and accept you, and therefore not hurt you because you are so amenable - you will lead an undemanding, easy life - you won't get into trouble: the chances of getting hurt will be low but you can't be sure - your decisions will be made for you	- you will get things done your way - you will bend people to your will - they will respect, even be afraid of you - you will hide any weaknesses by attacking them and exposing their own weaknesses - you will inspire confidence and progress in your career	- you will develop and maintain workable relationships with people - you will base these relationships on openness, trust, consistency of treatment, and on being an active listener - you will not accept that you are a target for manipulation or attack

Figure 3.2   Conscious and subconscious beliefs associated with each type of behaviour

13

25. What is your reaction to the descriptions in Figure 3.2? Which set of beliefs seem to describe better the aims of your own behaviour? Are these beliefs a distortion of the likely results as illustrated in Figure 3.3? Or are they an accurate reflection?

Submission	Aggression	Assertion
– you will be despised by many as lacking courage, not knowing your own mind, vacillating, weak and many more negative epithets – people will be continually frustrated in their dealings with you and will show it – you will not take control of your own destiny and your life will be drab, unexciting and friendless – you will lack personal integrity and self-esteem and your physical and mental health will suffer	– you will inspire antagonism, dislike, even fear in many people – you will attract extensive opposition from sturdier souls – your efforts will be nullified, even positively sabotaged, where the opportunity arises – people will not trust you – your stress level will be high – you will have an unrealistic view of your own integrity, and worse, you will be blissfully unaware of and reject any indications of the real situation – you stand a chance of being physically assaulted	– you will manage potentially stressful situations more effectively – you will extend your self-confidence and inspire confidence in others – you will avoid manipulation by others and deflect attack – you will have a realistic view of your own integrity and will make every effort to ensure it remains intact – you will maintain and exude a sense of well-being

Figure 3.3   Likely results of the behaviour

26. Having reflected on your responses to this checklist, what possible action could you take to develop yourself? Are there elements of submissive or aggressive behaviour which you want to eliminate?

27. What specifically should you do? And on further reflection, what will you do? Over what time-scale? How will you monitor your progress? And who else could be involved? Who should be involved?

28. Will you record your commitment to development? And genuinely assess your progress? How often?

29. If you are not prepared to do anything having answered the previous questions, what are you saying about yourself? Do you believe the answer? Are you truly happy with it? Are you sure?

4 Assertiveness: Strengthening the skills

Having taken the action you considered necessary to become more assertive (see Checklist 3) it may be helpful to check periodically whether you are maintaining progress. Such analyses will help you to strengthen your existing skills and provide a basis for any further action you consider appropriate. The following questions are designed to help you start the process.

1. What action, if any, have you taken as a result of reading Checklist 3?

2. To what extent do you find yourself still being either submissive or aggressive in particular social situations? Have you behaved in the following ways at any time in the past month and, if so, how often?

i   Standing up for yourself without upsetting people
ii   Losing your temper with people
iii   Admitting when you don't know the answer to a question
iv   Feeling embarrassed when somebody compliments you
v   Feeling you have been made to look a little foolish by what someone says to you
vi   Declining what you believe to be unreasonable demands or requests made of you, without upsetting people
vii   Prompting others to make decisions for you
viii   Fighting back when you are criticized
ix   Insisting on your rights as a customer or employee without being discourteous or offensive
x   Feeling you have to put people in their place
xi   Offering advice on what people ought to do in particular situations
xii   Feeling your self-respect is threatened by what some people say to you
xiii   Saying self-critical things to people (e.g. 'I'm just no good at that', 'I'm useless at drawing', 'I'm hopeless with figures')

xiv   Feeling resentful at the way some people treat you
xv   Being proud that you are one of life's competitors
xvi   Apologizing for what you have said or done
xvii   Finding people get irritated with you
xviii   Finding you have to criticize people for what they say
xix   Interrupting people as they are speaking
xx   Feeling you are in control of your life

Note: You probably know your IQ. You could begin to assess your AQ (Assertiveness Quotient) by scoring your responses to the 20 questions above. For questions 1, 3, 6, 9, and 20, score 5 each time you answered 'almost always', 4 for 'often', 3 for 'sometimes', 2 for 'rarely' and 1 for 'almost never'. For all remaining questions reverse your scores (5 for 'almost never', 4 for 'rarely', 3 for 'sometimes', 2 for 'often', and 1 for 'almost always).

3.   What do your answers suggest about the ways in which you have actually behaved in the past month? Do you want to become more assertive? In which particular ways?

     − Dealing with criticism of what you do?
     − Dealing with criticism of what you are?
     − Initiating and accepting discussions of both your strengths and limitations?
     − Actively prompting criticism?
     − Becoming a better listener?
     − Recognizing the signals in conversation which indicate what is concerning the speaker?
     − Making your point of view heard without getting stressed?

4.   Would it help to consider whether you could develop your approach to dealing more effectively with these (potentially stressful) situations? How often do you use the type of response shown in Figure 4.1?

5.   Having reflected on the responses illustrated in Figure 4.1, do you respond similarly without apologizing? Do you, can you, accept appropriate criticism, absorb sarcasm and verbal bullying *without becoming defensive*? Or aggressive?

6.   If you can develop this approach to dealing with potentially stressful situations do you recognize that by doing so you are giving yourself every chance to control your life positively, to be your own person?

7.   So what are you proposing to do now? Over the next week? The next month? A longer period?

Situation	Response
Criticism of your actions	'Yes, perhaps you're right' 'Yes, it does look like as if I might have made a mistake there' 'No, perhaps I shouldn't have done that'
Criticism of your personality	'That's true, I can upset some people' 'Yes, I accept that I am insensitive on occasions'
Prompting discussion which extends your self-knowledge	'I am rather concerned about what will happen when . . .' 'In that meeting, I felt that . . .' 'I don't know the answer to that one'
Prompting criticism	'What is it particularly about me that upsets you?' 'Is there anything else you would like to say about me?'
Becoming a better listener	'From what you were saying just now . . .' 'You feel that . . .' 'It seems to you that . . .'
Making your voice heard whilst remaining cool	'I understand what you're saying, but I feel that . . .' 'I appreciate that, but I still feel that . . .' 'Yes, I appreciate your difficulties, but I still feel that . . .'

Figure 4.1   Framing your responses

5 Coaching

The ability and willingness to give guidance and help to staff is an integral part of every manager's role: ability to assess accurately what coaching is appropriate, and willingness to commit time and effort to its achievement. It is this latter factor — willingness — which demands particular self-discipline. It is all too easy to allow good intentions to be buried under other, seemingly more pressing, tasks.

1. If you are a successful manager, what have been the significant factors in your success? Was one factor the positive help (guidance, coaching, counselling) you received from senior managers?

   - Are you still getting, or would you benefit from, further help now?
   - What does this answer indicate?

2. How seriously do managers in your organization take their responsibilities for developing staff?

   - Are they really aware of the implications of this responsibility?
   - How do you know?

3. Are they devoting as much time as they should to developing the performance of their staff? Are you?

   - To what extent is 'coaching' regarded as an integral part of every management job?
   - Do all managers help to develop the performance of their staff by:
     - Systematically giving them planned tasks to increase their abilities and experience?
     - Evaluating their performance in relation to these planned tasks?
     - Giving appropriate *personal* guidance to sustain/develop progress towards the target?
     - Generally monitoring performance against the time-scale set?
   - If not, what action is indicated?

4. Has a check ever been made in the organization to establish just how much training individual managers have received in coaching techniques?

   - How many individuals have attended practical training sessions outside the organization on the subject? Have any been conducted inside the organization?
     - How many work days were involved last year? How many so far this year? Spread over how many managers?
   - Is that really enough when the critical importance of *every* individual's contribution to success is considered?

5. If the (further) commitment of managers to the advantages of coaching is to be gained, has the practical application of the technique in your organization been fully explored?

   - If so, by whom? With what results?
   - If not, who should be responsible for doing so?

6. Have the following question areas been explored?

Strategy

7. What are the main areas within individual departments which could provide opportunities for coaching?

   The work itself

   - What are the main problems currently? Potentially?
   - Which can be used to provide a practical learning situation for staff?
   - Have the opportunities for coaching been positively identified?
   - Can targets (end states) be derived from these opportunities and closely specified?

   Individual staff

   - What shortcomings in attitudes, skills and/or knowledge have been identified, and need to be overcome?
   - Can targets for improvement/development be specified?

8. Can coaching priorities be set, based on the above?

Tactics

9. Considering the priorities in order, what action is appropriate to meet individual learning needs in terms of:

   - The situation itself?
     - What pre-planning is necessary?

- Will the relevance and value of the assignment be made absolutely clear? How?
  - The personality/skills of the manager concerned?
    - Interpersonal skills?
    - Listening skills?
  - The personality of the individual concerned?
    - Existing skills and knowledge?
    - General capability?

10. What timing and specific coaching approach do these answers suggest?

    - What will be delegated? How? When?
    - Will the appropriate authority to act be given?

Control

11. How will progress towards the targets be measured? What yardsticks are appropriate? What feedback is necessary?

    - Will the control be flexible and amenable to modification?
    - How will each individual's thinking be stimulated? Can the control be by watchful neglect?
    - Could such an approach help to build a sense of trust?
    - Will each individual be given every chance to monitor his or her own progress?

Further action

12. If managers are committed to this approach, would it be worthwhile evaluating individual managers' use of coaching by periodically asking them the following questions? And asking these questions of yourself?

    - What positive plans have you for coaching each one of your staff in the next six months?
    - What lessons have you learned from recent coaching situations? Are you applying them now?
      - Has your own management style developed?
    - What benefits has coaching produced in your department?
      - How does individual performance now compare with what it was six months ago? Twelve months ago?
    - If it has not improved markedly, are you really spending enough of your time on coaching?
    - Do you truly believe that by helping your own staff to grow you are growing yourself? If not, what does this answer indicate about your own managerial prospects (see question 1)?

6 Corporate culture

The tone of an organization – illustrated by the ways things are done, how people behave, the ceremonies and rituals – plays a vital role in shaping people's expectations. Understanding the nature of your own organization's culture, and its impact on day-to-day operations, is an important ingredient in the decisions you take.

Background analysis

1. What does 'corporate culture' mean in your organization?

    – To you?
    – To top management?
    – To supervisors and managers at different levels?
    – To everyone else?

2. To what extent do these views differ? How do you know?

    – Has a check ever been made?
    – If so, when was it last made?
    – Is a further check necessary now?

3. Could anyone in your organization have made the following comments?

    – 'Corporate culture? What's that?'
    – 'There's no such thing.'
    – 'This company is heading for trouble. The culture is wrong.'
    – 'Attitudes in this place are fossilized.'
    – 'Don't ask me, I only work here.'
    – 'We don't need 'culture'. We know what we've got to do.'
    – 'Our culture is simply that management is scared stiff of him upstairs.'
    – 'Talk about culture . . . There's only one person who makes decisions in this place.'
    – 'Culture is important, but what can we do about it?'

4. How important is it for the decision-takers on your organization to be absolutely clear about the impact of 'culture' on your organization?

    — Can you identify the 'shared meanings' in your organization? The accepted values? The beliefs about what is important? The sayings people use? The ways in which things get done?

5. How critical are these 'shared meanings' to the way you do your job? To the ways others do their jobs?

    — Are people agreed on why the organization exists?
    — How far do people at different levels agree what is of fundamental importance to your organization?

6. Whatever your answers, what is being done to ensure that the organization's culture is appropriate to today's environment? And to tomorrow's?

Diagnosing the prevailing culture

7. What is your organization about?

    — What are its objectives? Growth? Profit? Customer satisfaction? Market share? Product development? Service excellence? Survival? Or what?
    — What is the view of top management?
    — What are the views of managers at different levels?
    — What are the views of everyone else?

    Do these views fit with the culture the organization is trying to foster?

8. What seems to be the top priority for the 'foot soldiers' in your organization?

    — Staying out of the firing line?
    — Doing a good job?
    — Pushing for more money or promotion?
    — Keeping their jobs?

    What is the organization's view on these issues? How has it been made known?

9. What are the general expectations within the organization in terms of:

    — Behaviour?
    — Dress?
    — Timekeeping?
    — Acceptance of authority?
    — Work performance?

    What other 'marks of acceptance' are there? What does this tell you about the 'tone' of the organization?

10. What are regarded as personal virtues by the organization? Achievement? Survival? Integrity? Loyalty? Honesty? Self-sacrifice? Being behind a desk? Hard work? Commitment? Or what?

    − Again, what does your answer tell you about the 'tone' of the organization?

11. What special language is used?

    − What initials or other jargon is used?
    − What technical language is used?
    − What is the official motto?
    − What is the unofficial motto?

    Why do members of the organization use this special language?

12. What are the organization's rituals and ceremonies? Parties? Outings? Long-service presentations? Other events? Ways of doing things? What do they tell you about the way in which the organization sees itself?

13. How do people feel that they are regarded by the organization?

    − Do they regard themselves as exchanging their labour for pay?
    − Do they feel part of a family?
    − Do they feel part of a community?
    − Do they see themselves merely as sellers in a market-place? If not, how do they see themselves?

14. What status distinctions are there? Separate dining rooms? Special parking spaces? Other privileges? Access to secretarial and other resources?

    − How do people feel about them?

15. Does the organization have heroes?

    − Why are they regarded as heroic?
    − What does this tell you about the culture?

16. How positive have your answers been to these questions?

    − What does the strength of your response indicate about your organization's culture?
    − What would prevent a newcomer from being accepted?
    − What would result in an existing employee being 'cold shouldered'?
    − Just how strongly are beliefs and values held?

17. Do these beliefs and values apply across the entire organization?

    − Do they apply across particular divisions/departments?

    Or are they peculiar to specific work groups?

Cultural 'fit'

18. Does the prevailing culture enhance your organization's performance?

    — How particularly does it help?
    — Does it help corporate goals to be achieved?
    — Does it make communication easier?
    — Does it encourage greater co-operation?
    — Are staff motivated to perform more effectively? How?

19. Or does the culture hinder performance?

    — How prevalent is 'group think'?
    — Is there any noticeable entrenched resistance to change?
      Or to concealment of bad news?

    In what other ways might the culture detract from corporate goals?

20. What steps are being taken now to ensure that the values of prospective entrants fit the organizational culture?

    — What values, attitudes or beliefs would exclude a candidate during the selection process?
    — How are key values conveyed to the candidate?

21. To what extent do new entrants suffer from 'culture-shock'?

    — Is this contributing to an induction crisis?
    — What action, if any, does your answer suggest?

22. How are new entrants inducted into the culture?

    — Through a formal programme?
    — Through a staff handbook?
    — Informally by talking to old-hands?
    — Picking it up as they go along?

    Is a system of 'mentoring' operated? If so, how were the mentors chosen? What criteria were used?

23. In your organization, how are cultural values communicated? Through memos? Through the company newspaper? Employee reports? Meetings? Rewards (e.g. promotion, recognition)? Punishments (e.g. being passed over, demoted)? By the actions of management?

    — Or how?
    — In what other significant ways are these values communicated?

24. What is the attitude within the organization towards 'mavericks' who publicly behave contrary to cultural expectations?

    — Are they ignored? Are they isolated? Are they encouraged? Are they tolerated?
    — How precisely are they treated?

Cultural development

25. Is there a need for cultural change?

    – Just how much is company policy resisted?
    – In what particular ways is it resisted?
    – Is there a ready explanation for such attitudes?
    – How do people feel about the introduction of new technology?
    – To what extent is the current level of productivity acceptable?

    In general terms, would you say that morale is high? Or does it need to be improved?

26. How well do people cope with any changes now? Do they fear change? Or do they welcome it? Do they accept it as inevitable? What does your answer say about the way the organization operates?

27. How are the advantages of changes put to people?

    – Are the likely repercussions of any changes reviewed before the event? Are you sure? How do you know?
    – What more could be done in the future to ensure such reviews are more effective?
    – Who should be involved? Are they?

28. How could such change be introduced?

    – By example? Whose example would be particularly appropriate?
    – By coercion? Have the implications of such an approach been thought through fully?
    – By reward? What methods specifically would achieve the desired result?
    – By persuasion?
    – By participation/involvement?

29. During discussions on strategic change is the prevailing culture within the organization considered fully? Are the cultural implications of tactical decisions also considered in detail?

    – Is the culture appropriate for involving people fully in deciding the particular parameters of any changes?
    – What would happen if people do not co-operate, particularly as a result of poor communication?
    – What are the wider implications of your answers to these questions?

30. How much influence do you personally have in shaping the way in which your organization operates?

    – What action does your answer suggest?

31. How does this review of the way your organization operates affect your role as a human resource development specialist?

    − How can you utilize your understanding to promote the cause of human resource development in your organization?

32. What action on your part is appropriate? How soon should such action be taken? Within what time frame?

7 Costing human assets

Annual company reports refer to the salary costs of employing staff, although relatively few seem to record other costs relating to employment. Some European companies, for instance, specify not only the year's training costs but also the number and proportion of staff who have received training. The costs of training, absenteeism, staff turnover and accidents at work are all factors contributing to corporate success or failure, yet for the most part seem to remain hidden. The accuracy of this assertion can be easily tested: using the headings in the checklist, compare the *total* cost of employing staff in the last financial year in your organization with the figure included in its annual report.

Background considerations

1. To what extent could the number of employees in your organization be cut back before a significant reduction in productivity became noticeable? Are you certain there is no unnecessary duplication of effort/overlapping of functions?

2. Allowing for the particular nature of your organization's business, is the ratio of full-time to part-time employees realistic? What is the current proportion of directs to indirects? How much did subcontract labour cost in the last financial year?

3. How often are these figures reviewed? By whom? When was the last time a review took place?

4. Are the following specific areas of human assets costs examined regularly.

Human resource planning

5. When new projects and technological developments are mooted, is

the 'people' element fully scrutinized? And fully costed? Is sufficient emphasis given to this factor? Are you sure?

6. What changes to staffing levels have been forecast? Over what time scale(s)?

7. How much will the changes cost/save?

8. Below what annual percentage rate are staff costs constrained now?

9. What is the planned future position?

10. Is everyone responsible aware of the long-term cost implications of the proposed changes in staff numbers?

Recruitment and selection

11. Are your organization's recruitment and selection procedures cost effective? Are you sure?

12 Are you aware of how much the various recruitment media used are costing your organization? If not, what action is indicated? When?

13. Are the most cost-effective selection techniques used? Are you sure? How recently has an evaluation been conducted?

14. What is the per capita cost of placement at the moment?
    Is that too high?
    What plans are there for reducing it?

15. Are you getting value for money? How do you know?

16. What efforts are being made currently to locate new more cost-effective sources of candidates? And to develop more effective selection techniques?

17. In view of the increasing impact of information technology, what consideration is being given to introducing or extending the use of contracts-for-work (also known as contracts-for-service), rather than contracts-of-work (using the services of self-employed 'out-workers')? Has a potential cost-benefit analysis been conducted recently? If not, what action is indicated?

Training

18. What was your organization's total wage/salary bill in the last financial year? What was sales turnover in the same period?

19. How does direct training expenditure compare with each of these figures? How do the proportions compare with the previous year? And the year before that? What proportions are planned for next year? In each case, is that enough to ensure success? Against what criteria?

20. What is the current figure for indirect training expenditure (wages/salaries of training staff, etc.)? Is this expenditure truly productive? How do you know?

21. Bearing the above figures in mind, how cost-effective do you think your organization's training is now? What proportion of the training budget is devoted to evaluating the effectiveness of training activities? Is that really sufficient? And if evaluation efforts are unsatisfactory, what immediate action is indicated? By whom?

22. What plans are there for achieving greater cost effectiveness in the future? Are all those involved fully in the picture? Are you sure?

23. For instance, how much is the induction of new employees currently costing your organization? How cost effective is it? If the figures cannot be identified what should be done? When? By whom?

24. Are the costs of other types of training identified accurately? What proportional contribution does each make to your organization's performance? Is the balance right? Are you sure?

25. What are the organization's training priorities now? How have they been decided? Who decided them? In consultation with who else? Viewed against the organization's bottom-line performance, are the priorities realistic?

26. In broad terms, can you show that there is a positive pay-off from the training activities currently undertaken? And for the planned future activity?

27. Just how far is training activity in your organization focused currently on efficiency (doing things right) as opposed to effectiveness (doing the right things)? To re-emphasize the question, to what extent does your organization's training activity really contribute to overall corporate performance? Is the organization truly getting its money's worth?

Staff utilization

28. What is the current relationship between actual and possible hours worked (the productive/possible person-hours ratio)? What has been the trend over the last three years?

29. Are the factors affecting this ratio continuously reviewed? What was the outcome of the latest review? What should be done now?

Safety

30. What was the financial cost to your organization of accidents during the last year? Were the following costs included in the figure?

   - Supervisory/management time on replanning?
   - Lost production?
   - Sub-contracting?

   If the cost cannot be identified readily, what needs to be done? How soon?

31. What is being done currently to make accident prevention more effective? Is this sufficient? Against what criteria?

Staff benefits

32. Are cost breakdowns prepared on the various staff benefits provided by the organization? If not, what should be done? If so,

   - Who reviews these costs?
   - At what intervals?
   - Is that often enough?

33. When was the last time a cost/benefit analysis was conducted? Should a further analysis be conducted now? By whom?

Wages/salaries

34. What is the current annual cost to the organization of wages/salaries?

35. Are individual employees paid according to their contribution to the organization? In terms of the worth of the jobs themselves and individual effectiveness in performing them? Are you sure?

36. What have been the trends in recent years by occupation, grade, etc? What are the likely future trends? Are earnings projections made? How often are they reviewed? By whom?

37. Are any financial incentive schemes in operation regularly reviewed? When was the last time? Are you sure any gradual loosening is being checked?

38. Is overtime a significant factor in your organization's operations?

   - Is that level of overtime really necessary?
   - What was the cost of overtime payments during the last quarter? During the last financial year?

- How do these figures compare with the previous periods? What is the trend?
- What proportion of the total wages/salaries bill is accounted for by overtime payments? Is it rising/steady/falling?
- What action do these answers suggest? Who should take it? When?

39. What is the current cost of employing temporary workers? What has been the trend over the last three years? What is the projected cost for the next financial year? Is that figure realistic or is a gradual loosening of control taking place? What action is indicated to improve control of this?

Absenteeism

40. Do you know the current cost of absenteeism in your organization?

41. Have you costed the effect of absenteeism on:
    - Production?
    - Scrap/waste levels?
    - Machine downtime?
    - Late deliveries?
    - Rescheduling time by management?

42. What needs to be done to minimize this effect? What further needs to be done? By whom? How soon?

Staff wastage

43. How much is staff wastage costing your organization? Has the true economic cost been considered? Does the costing include the following factors:
    - Loss of leaver's skill?
    - Loss of output?
    - Recruitment and selection replacements?
    - Training (including induction) expenses?
    - Higher scrap/wastage during training?
    - General administrative expenses?

    If not, what needs to be done? When? By whom?

Industrial relations

44. How many man-days were lost in your organization in the last financial year as a result of industrial action? What was the cost in terms of lost production? Lost orders?

45.   What efforts are being made currently to improve the cost effectiveness of your organization's industrial relations practices? Is that effort sufficient? Are you sure?

46.   If any of the above factors require attention in your organization, what does this signify about existing staff competence/liaison? Who should do what? After consultation with who else?

8   Delegation

Managers who do not delegate tasks will fail themselves, their staff, and the organization they represent. Attempting everything personally, they feel harassed and overworked despite ever-increasing effort.

To break this vicious circle requires self-discipline: it can often seem easier to do jobs which may take longer to explain than complete. The discipline lies in overcoming this selfishness to consider the needs of staff who want to grow, to feel they are getting somewhere. Unless the right tasks are delegated to the right people at the right time, they will not grow — and neither will you.

Preliminary diagnosis

1. To what extent do you plan your job? Does it have any tendency to plan you?

2. How effectively do you manage your time? Whatever your response, are you sure you know?

3. Do you take work home regularly?

4. Do you work much longer hours than your staff?

5. Do you have difficulties in meeting deadlines?

6. Do you spend too much time on detail?

7. Do people come to you too often for instructions on:
    - What should be done?
    - When it should be done?
    - How it should be done?
    - Who should do it?
    - Where it should be done?
    - Why it should be done?

34

8. Where is your personal stress threshold now? In front of you? Behind you? In either case, how far away is it?

9. What are the strengths, weaknesses, opportunities and threats presented by your current workload?

    − Take a critical 'snapshot' now: to what extent are you achieving your major accountabilities? What are your strong points? What are the flaws in your personal productivity? Currently? Potentially? How could your answers be used to consolidate your position? Or be used against you?

10. What action is suggested by your answers to these questions? To what extent could a more effective distribution of work ease the burden?

11. Could your present approach to delegating tasks be modified or extended? Should it? Just how far would you like to improve?

Preparing to delegate

12. Which parts of your work could, and should, be delegated? Have you thought through the possibilities? In detail? What tasks can you identify?

13. In the context of overall section/department activities, how important is each one?

14. Who should do what? Can you match the task to the person? The person to the task?

    The task itself

    − What are the priorities within the task?
    − Within what time frame must the task be completed?
    − What are the cost limits?
    − What resources can be called on?
    − What additional information will be needed?
    − What potential problems might arise? Who should deal with them?
    − What decisions must be referred back?
    − What contingency planning is necessary?

    The person

    − Does the task require a particular level of existing skills, knowledge or attitudes.
    − Is the task being used to provide a valuable learning experience?
    − Who could, and would, benefit most from involvement/ responsibility?
    − How does the task fit into the person's current workload?

- Are you clear about why you are delegating to the person concerned?
- Is the degree of risk acceptable?

Taking action

15. What approach is most appropriate?

Location

- Where should the task be delegated?
  - Where others can hear?
  - Where others should hear?
  - In private?

Timing

- When should the task be delegated?
  - What would be the best moment?

Method

- How should the task be delegated?
  - Verbally?
  - Or in writing?
  - If verbally, is a request or an instruction most appropriate?

Focus of briefing

- Will the briefing concentrate on the critical parameters of the task? And on personal accountability for results?
- What degree of planning by the person independently will be appropriate?
- How much flexibility should be built into the task?
- Is 'watchful neglect' appropriate? Or should the control be tighter?
- Will you delegate the right to be wrong?
- Will necessary monitoring arrangements be agreed? And followed subsequently?
- Will a date/time be fixed for the debriefing/feedback session?

Communication net

- Who needs to know what you have delegated and to whom? Who might it also be useful to inform?

Follow up

16. What was the effect of your delegation?

On the person concerned

- How well was the task performed?
- What future coaching/counselling needs can be identified?
- What was the reaction to your feedback?
- What action does your answer suggest?

On other staff

- What have been their reactions?

On yourself

- In broad terms did your preparation produce the results you wanted?
- Did you match the task to the person effectively?
- Did you save time? Did you use the saving productively?
- What action on your part do your answers suggest?

17. What have you learned which will be helpful in delegating tasks in the future? How will you make sure that the learning is not forgotten for the next time?

9 Designing jobs

Whilst at a strategic level the design of individual jobs must be integrated with corporate plans, there are also a number of issues which are significant tactically. Such issues include the degree of autonomy, the opportunities for advancement and the influence of new technology.

A critical appraisal of the content of jobs in your organization may well identify areas for improvement.

Background considerations

1. Is your organization concerned about:
    - Administrative overload?
    - Labour turnover?
    - Absenteeism?
    - Unfair pay policies?
    - Missed deadlines/targets?
    - Accident rates?
    - Introduction of new technology?
    - Wastage/rework rates?
    - Inefficient work scheduling?
    - Unequal distribution of workloads?
    - Low morale?
    - Customer complaints?

    Or any other factors which may indicate that people are not giving their best?

2. Is there any indication that the content of individual jobs affects the above factors?

3. Is it possible that an analysis of individual jobs might form the starting point from which to improve the situation?

4. Have such analyses ever been conducted in your organization? If so, why was the decision made? Who was responsible for conducting the

analyses? How was this person chosen? By whom?

5. What were the outcomes of any analyses? Did they improve the situation? If so, how? If not, why not?

6. Is it part of every departmental manager's job to assess how the context of individual jobs could be improved? Should it be? Or should there be one person who has the overall responsibility within the organization for designing jobs?

The organization's objectives

7. Is all the necessary background information (marketing data, financial considerations, etc.) realistically assessed before strategic corporate objectives are formulated? And before associated tactical planning takes place? Are people at all levels made aware of these objectives? Should they be? Would it help if they were to be made more aware?

8. At which stage in the planning process is the design of individual jobs considered?

   – Before, during, or after the objectives have been chosen?
   – Continuously during the planning process?

9. Is the design of individual jobs integrated with the organization's plans for the future? Or is design conducted on an *ad hoc* basis? What action, if any, does your answer suggest?

10. How are tasks grouped to form particular jobs?

    – Against what criteria?
      • Organizational effectiveness?
      • Organizational efficiency?
      • People's preferences?
      • A match between these criteria?
    – Has the grouping been done systematically?
      • How do you know?

11. Is it part of your organization's approach to job design that individual jobs should be subservient to machines? That jobs should be de-skilled?

12. Is this approach realistic in the broadest sense? Have the human implications been considered fully? Should total cost be considered as a criterion rather than merely direct cost? For instance, what are the effects on morale, absenteeism, etc, if the skill element in jobs is minimized?

13. What effect may these factors be having on the total cost of your organization's products or services?

39

14. Is advantage taken of new technology to enhance jobs?

Job design

General considerations

15. Could the job embrace work done currently by other people? Could parts of the job done by people be done by machines?

16. What would be the advantages of so doing in terms of:
    - Minimizing the repetitive elements of work to release people for more meaningful work?
    - Enlarging the scope of individual jobs?
    - Improving quality and reliability?

Significance

17. How could the individual job be made more meaningful to the job holder? In terms of contribution to product/utilities or service excellence? In other terms? For instance could job holders be made more aware of the cost implications of their work? The quality implications? Would such awareness lead to improved commitment and involvement?

Variety/autonomy

18. Could the job holder be allowed more discretion to use his or her authority in:
    - Setting personal targets?
    - Planning the most effective ways of meeting these targets (e.g. setting personal standards)?
    - Measuring personal performance in meeting the targets?
    - Making changes in job methods, timing, use of resources, etc. to improve productivity?

Communication

19. In what ways could involvement and participation be increased?
    - Is the amount and level of communication appropriate?
    - Could communication channels be improved?
    - Is the right method of communication used?
      - Would briefing groups help?
    - Could the job holder become more involved in formulating procedures? (For example, on operational safety procedures.)

Relationships

20. Could the opportunity for membership of a work group be extended? How?
    − What would be the advantages of extending the current level of support?

Feedback controls

21. How could the job be modified to provide more challenge, either administratively or technically? For instance, could periodic reports be made available directly to the person concerned so that the results of personal efforts may be identified?

    − What is the current impact of performance review (appraisal) discussions?

Opportunity for advancement

22. Could the provision of opportunities for advancement (a career progression structure) be extended to reward high performance?

23. How are good staff motivated when promotion possibilities are limited?

Impact of new technology

24. How has new technology influenced individual jobs in the recent past? What is its influence currently?

    − What training needs have been identified already?
    − What training needs are being identified now?
    − What are the foreseeable future needs?
    − How have ways of working changed? What further changes are likely?
    − What has been the effect on career planning? What will be the likely future effect?

25. As a human resources development specialist what more could you do to influence the design of jobs in your organization? What more should you do? What actions do your answers suggest?

10 Evaluating a learning event

Evaluation of learning events tends to take place unsystematically, if at all. Insufficient thought is devoted to evaluating the role of the evaluation process itself in clarifying and modifying the perceptions of those involved. How many of the training and development programmes conducted in your organization over the past twelve months have been thoroughly evaluated?

1. What does the word 'evaluation' mean to you in the context of a learning event?

2. Who do you believe should decide the worth of the events you conduct?

    – Is evaluation, however you define it, your responsibility?
    – Is it the responsibility of individual participants?
    – Or is it a joint responsibility? Or someone else's responsibility?

3. Apart from yourself, who contributes to the psychological contract associated with a particular event? Merely the participants? Or others as well? Who, specifically, are the stakeholders? Should *all* stakeholders be involved in any evaluation? If not, can you justify your stance? On what grounds, specifically?

4. What do you believe should be evaluated in the events you conduct? All the main elements? Or just some? Or something else?

    – Again, how can you justify such a stance?
    – Do you view learning events as part of a continuing process? Or merely as a product? Or does your perspective combine both process and product?
    – Is any distinction drawn between the following educational element(s) in the events you conduct?

	Element		*Focus*
●	Instruction	●	Knowledge
●	Training	●	Skill
●	Initiation	●	Attitudes

– Does your evaluation design vary according to each different focus of learning? Are those people identified by your response to question 3 involved in the design? If not, why not?

5. How should any evaluation be achieved? Using what particular approach (or approaches) to evaluation?

6 When should the evaluation take place? Should the principle be established before the event? Established and conducted afterwards? Within what time frame? Are you sure your answer makes sense? To you? To others? (See Figure 10.1)

7. What do your answers suggest about the way you approach evaluation?

– How did you come to hold such views? Having considered your response, to what extent do you believe your views on this aspect of learning reflect your own personal values and beliefs? Just how far should they?

– To what extent could your biases and prejudices be actively discouraging, rather than encouraging, learning in others? (After all, your prejudices are only your values under another name.)

8. What is your focus of interest now in evaluating the learning events in which you are involved?

– At what level of generality does evaluation take place? Is it genuinely more thoughtful than the 'happiness rating' completed at the conclusion of some learning events?

9. To what extent are you familiar with the various approaches to evaluation? What evaluation 'labels' would you associate with the following questions?

– What is the worth of this learning event? Should we be concerned with it at all?

– Are 'end-states' important? Or is the process of discovery, and self-discovery, more important? Who should decide?

– How should the learning methods used during the event be questioned? Should they be questioned? By whom?

– In what ways could the questions raised in any evaluation of this event be explored? Who should explore them?

– Would sociological insights and approaches be useful?

– How should the different perceptions and needs of those involved be accommodated?

– Could the role conflict of an evaluator as a team member in this event be utilized?

	Purpose	Design	Implementation	Evaluation

What	– What are the learners needs?
	– What should be the purpose of the learning event?
	– Is the learning for
	  • Maintenance?
	  • Change?
	– What mix of instruction, training and initiation is appropriate?
	– What constraints (time, cost, etc.) must be taken into account?
		– What is the focus of learning?
		– What factors should be taken into account in the design of the event?
		– What methods would be most effective in meeting the purpose? In what mix?
		– What is the environment in which the design will be implemented?
			– What factors should be considered in implementing the design?
			– What should be the role of the trainer?
				– What evaluation should there be?
				– What methods should be used?
				– What alternatives are there?
				– What should be evaluated?
				  • Purpose?
				  • Design?
				  • Implementation?
				  • Evaluation?

Why	– Why those needs?
	– Why that purpose?
	– Is the purpose justifiable?
	  • Practical?
	  • Realistic?
	  • Within the constraints that apply?
		– Why that focus?
		– Why that design?
		– Is it creative?
		– Is it capable of iteration?
			– Why that approach?	– Why that particular approach to evaluation?
				– Why that emphasis?
				– Why those priorities?

Who	– Who should decide the purpose of the learning? Who are the learners? Trainers? Participants? Both?	– Who should decide the design? – In consultation with who else?	– Who should be involved in the implementation?	– Who should be involved in the evaluation? – What should be the role of the trainer? Participants?

Figure 10.1 Evaluating a learning event: some questions

	Purpose	Design	Implementation	Evaluation
	− What is their perspective on learning? What are their character-istics as people? Who are they?			
Why	− Why that person? − Why those people?	− Why that person? − Why those people?	− Why that person? − Why those people?	− Why that person? − Why those people?
How	− How should the purpose be decided?	− How should the design be decided?	− How should the approach be implemented? • Structure? • Sequence? • Methods?	− How should the evaluation be carried out?
Why	− Why in that way?	− Why in that way?	− Why in that way?	− Why in that way?
When	− When should the purpose be decided? • Before the event? • During the event? • At some other time? When?	− When should the design be decided? • Before the event? • During the event? − When should the methods be decided?	− When should the approach be implemented?	− When should the evaluation be carried out?
Why	− Why then?	− Why then?	− Why then?	− Why then?

Figure 10.1 *concluded*

- Does feedback need to be cheap and fast? Is the need realistic? From whose point of view?
- How much has the event cost? How much would the preferred approach to evaluating the event cost?
- Could a value-free position be adopted during any evaluation of the unintended results of the event?

10. Is the identification of the appropriate label important to you? If so, why? If identification is less important, again, why?

11. What do all your answers to these questions suggest about your present involvement in, and commitment to, the process of evaluation? Do you feel you know enough? Do you practice it? What more could you do?

12. What action should you take now to develop your contribution to the learning events in which you are involved?

13. What, if anything, do you actually propose to do? Over what time-scale? How will you evaluate your own progress?

11 Evaluating psychological tests

A valid ('does it do what it says it does?') and reliable ('does it do it ten times out of ten?') psychological test used in the right place at the right time for the right reasons can enhance the success of human resource development strategy in your organization. The problem lies in choosing the most appropriate measure to do the required job within your own circumstances. Basically the choice is between 'buying-in' from outside or developing your own 'in-house' measure – the decision depends upon which approach is the more cost-effective. Most of the following questions can be applied in either circumstance and are designed to help you review some of the critical parameters.

Purpose

1. Will the particular psychological test which you are considering, carry out more precisely the job which other methods do, for example interviewing?

2. Can its results be used to supplement and/or cross-check other data which you already possess?

3. What principal function will the test fulfil?
   - Will it be used to compare people?
   - Or will it be used to diagnose problems and difficulties?

4. What specific purpose will it serve? Will it be used to assist in selection and promotion decisions? To assess people's progress in training? To assist in counselling (for example, careers advice)? To evaluate the effectiveness of procedures (for example, selection, training programmes)? As part of a staff-appraisal procedure? As part of a research programme? Or on an exploratory basis to assess feasibility?

5. What does the test measure?

- Personality?
- Intelligence?
- Special aptitudes?
- Attitudes and opinions?
- Motivation and interests?

Validity and reliability

6. Does the test appear to be measuring the attribute(s) which are of interest you?

    - How detailed is the description offered by the test constructor?

7. Is there any written assurance that the items in the test or schedule cover adequately the attribute(s) you wish to measure?

8. Are there any details of its use in circumstances similar to your own, with similar people, and for similar purposes?

9. Is there strong statistical evidence that the test produces results which are comparable with other measures of the same attributes?

10. Has the test been used successfully to predict behaviour or performance?

11. Is there detailed statistical evidence to show that the test is reliable?

    - If the same test (or where there is more than one version, a second form) was used would the same sort of results be produced for the same, or a similar, group of participants?
    - Do people score consistently across all the items? (For example, do they get most of the difficult items wrong and most of the easier items right in a test of intelligence?)

Acceptability

12. Is there every assurance that the test does not discriminate unfairly? Or breach anti-discrimination legislation?

13. Would participants find it acceptable?

    - Would they have any strong reservations about the way the test is worded and presented?

Administration

14. How easy is the test/schedule to obtain and administer?

15. Is it supplied only to recognized or qualified practitioners?

16. Is training available for recognition to use the test?

    — Is training in test-use more economical than buying-in the test service from an agency?

17. What proportion of the test materials is reusable?

18. Can non-specialists set and score the test?

19. How long does the test take to administer?

20. Are there clear instructions as to the standard conditions for administering the test (for example, room conditions, instructions to participants)?

21. How long does it take to score the test?

    — Is it machine-scoreable?

22. Does it offer a single score? A number of scores, some of which you may ignore? A profile for a collection of attributes?

Interpretation

23. How will the scores be used?

    — On a pass/fail basis?
    — On a high-to-low score basis (i.e. above 70 per cent, 60 to 70 per cent, etc.)?
    — On a profile matching basis?

    How will you ensure that you have chosen the right pass level or profile for your purpose(s)?

24. Are there detailed instructions on interpreting the results?

    — Are there clear instructions on what the scores mean?

25. Is there a basis for comparing your results with others?

    — Are there figures to show how people similar to yours perform on the test?
    — Can you compare any individual from your sample with the general cross-section for all such individuals?
    — Do you know the average (mean) scores for these people?

Disclosure

26. What information, if any, on the results is to be disclosed to individual participants?

    — Have you thought through the implications of your answer?

27. In circumstances where participants will not be informed and/or the information is to be used for socially-sensitive decisions such as promotions, what assurance is there that faking or cheating is difficult?

Legal position

28. What is the legal position regarding the confidentiality and storage of the results?

Follow up

29. What steps should be taken to follow up the results, for instance by observing people's performance or behaviour subsequently or by comparing the results with other information, such as supervisors' reports?

Review

30. Having considered these questions on evaluating a particular psychological test, do you now intend to 'buy-in'? Or develop your own?

    - In either case what communications groundwork will be necessary to consult/inform those involved?
    - What may be the reaction of staff to the use of this test, particularly if it is for the first time? How will any negative fears/reactions be allayed?

    In brief, will the introduction be thought through effectively before the event? Or be the focus of embarrassment subsequently?

12 External training courses

Even in the best run organizations there is an occasional need to use external training courses. Alternative ways of meeting the need should be considered first, however, and if an external course seems most appropriate then every effort should be made to ensure a maximum return on the costs involved.

1. Have the training needs of the individual(s) concerned been identified? Precisely? For instance, if a supposed communications training need has been identified, what particular type of communication is involved? Verbal? Or written? If written, is the need to improve performance in writing memos, reports, business letters or what?

2. How was the need identified? Was it done by consultation? With the individual(s) concerned? By whom? If it was not immediate supervision, why?

3. Is the need for:
   - Initial training?
   - Booster training?
   - Retraining?

4. Having pinpointed the training need, have you also identified the standard of performance required as a result of the training? With those concerned? Have the criteria of success been established? Have these criteria been quantified where possible?

5. Once the parameters have been established, have you examined thoroughly all alternative methods of meeting the need? On a cost-effectiveness basis?

6. If, as a result, using an external training course appears to be the most effective means, have you considered the following points?

- How many staff need training?
- For how long?
- When should they be trained?
- What are the priorities?
- How should they be trained?
- Where should they be trained?
- At what cost?

7. Have you considered, on a cost-effectiveness basis, the possibility of mounting an in-company course with the help of outside speakers to fill the training need?

8. What would be the other advantages of this approach (e.g. a tailor-made course concentrating on your organization's policies/practices/needs.)?

9. If this approach is not appropriate, how do you choose the most suitable external course?

10. Does your organization maintain a 'register' of courses on offer at different levels and for different occupational groups?

11. Who is (or should be) responsible for its regular updating?

12. Are you aware of the various bodies which provide information on course availability (e.g. your industry's training board, regional management centre, the various professional institutes, research associations, etc.)? Is your organization on their mailing lists? If not, what action should be taken? By whom?

13. How is the effectiveness of particular external courses checked? If assessment does not take place prior to use, why not ?

14. When a particular course has been chosen, is the individual concerned briefed fully before attending the course? Is agreement reached with him or her on:

- Why attendance is necessary?
- What is expected in terms of pre-course preparation?
- What is expected during the course? And on return from the course?

15. When the individual returns from an external course is he or she asked to prepare a critical report on the course against the criteria of success established at the outset? If not, why not? If so, who is responsible for reviewing the feedback and following up with any necessary action? Is it done? By the right person?

16. During the last financial year, how many employee days were devoted to external training? How does this figure compare with that for training carried out within the organization? What were the total

costs of each type of training? How does each figure, and the total, compare with the organization's sales turnover in the same period? Was it too much? Or too little? Against what criteria?

17. Is your organization really getting its money's worth from using external courses?

13 Industrial relations

Whilst the maintenance of co-operative relationships at work is no easy task, it can be achieved more effectively if coherent policies on industrial relations issues are understood and accepted by those involved.

Training both managers and employee representatives will help to encourage a positive climate in which industrial relations problems are discussed.

Preliminary analysis

1. Has a written policy statement been prepared which indicates the organization's policy and attitudes towards industrial relations?

2. Are the organization's objectives on industrial relations for the short, medium and longer term known to all members of management? Who made them known? How? When?

3. Are the policy and objectives understood and accepted at all levels? How do you know? If there is any doubt about what should be done?

4. Do well-defined negotiating and consultative procedures exist within which the organization's industrial relations objectives are discussed? Do all levels of management have a working knowledge of these procedures? Are you sure?

5. Are the roles of, and the contacts between, each level of management and employee representatives within the procedures clearly defined and fully understood by them? If not, what should be done? By whom? When?

Management involvement

6. Does every manager in your organization understand the industrial

relations framework in the industry of which the organization is a part? Appreciate the implications and effects of the national industrial relations situation on the industry and the organization?

- Does every manager have personal copies of relevant industry or national codes? Do they also have personal copies of the organization's procedural agreements? Of substantive agreements (or easy access to them)?

Employee involvement

7. How many employee representatives (shop stewards) are there in your organization?

8. Do you know what their jobs as employee representatives are? Precisely? Are you sure? Do you also know to which particular unions they belong?

9. Can you identify the working groups for which individual representatives are responsible? Can everyone else? Again, are you sure?

10. Has a definition of the role of employee representatives been drawn up following consultation between the union(s) concerned and management? If not, why? If so, when was this done? Does it require updating?

11. Has agreement been reached between management and unions on the following issues?
    - Conditions of eligibility for election (e.g. minimum age, length of service)?
    - The text of written credentials indicating
      - The rights/duties of elected representatives?
      - Period of office?
      - Work group represented?
    - The publication of these credentials for the information of all concerned?
    - Time off during the working day to carry out union responsibilities?
    - Facilities to enable these responsibilities to be carried out (e.g. accommodation for meetings, telephone access, etc.)?
    - Identification and fulfilment of any training necessary to help representatives carry out their responsibilities effectively?
    - Maintenance of earnings whilst so doing? Or whilst attending training courses?

12. Is your organization complying with current industry or national recommendations on treatment of employee representatives? How do you know? Are you absolutely sure it is?

Communication channels

13.   Do effective communication channels exist by which all concerned are kept informed and, if appropriate, know who to contact on matters (particularly industrial relations issues) which affect them?

14.   How do you know that these channels are effective? What instances have occurred in the past year of communication failures which have caused problems of non-cooperation? What action was taken to rectify the situation? Was it effective? Whose responsibility is it to ensure continuing effectiveness?

15.   Have all levels of management received training in communication skills? Is booster training needed now? If not, how do you know?

Problem areas

16.   What particular industrial relations problem areas have been identified in the past year? Did they include any of the following?

   − Wage and salary systems?
   − Work of equal value?
   − Absenteeism?
   − Treatment of minority groups (e.g. discrimination against the disabled, ethnic minorities, etc.)?
   − Staff turnover?
   − Health, safety and welfare?
   − Inequality of opportunities (arising from gender, sexual orientation, age, etc.)?
   − Grievance issues being taken regularly beyond the initial stages?
   − Sexual harassment?
   − Number of disputes?
   − Staff dismissals?

   What action has been taken to reduce their incidence? Was it effective? Against what criteria? What is your organization's stance on these and other similar problems? Are you complying with the law? And have policy statements been prepared? Are such statements readily available to all concerned? If not, what action is indicated?

Responsibility

17.   What do you judge to be the focus of potential industrial relations problems over the next year? The following year? What action is necessary, in your view, to minimize their possible impact?

18.   Whose responsibility is it to identify potential problem areas in industrial relations? Is this responsibility understood and accepted? Are you sure?

The future

19. Are any changes in the organization's industrial relations policies and practices planned in the foreseeable future?

   - Who will make the final decision on the changes? After consultation with whom?
   - How will the changes be implemented?
   - Will all those involved be consulted/informed before the event? How?
   - What will be the effect on the training needs of all levels of management? Other staff groups?

20. In fact, what is the organization's current/planned commitment to training on any aspect of industrial relations for:

   - All levels of management?
   - Employee representatives?
   - All other employees?

   Is that sufficient when compared with the answers to the previous questions? If not, what should be done to rectify the situation forthwith?

21. For instance, what training has been undertaken to ensure that all concerned are fully aware on a 'need to know' basis of current industrial relations legislation? Is that sufficient in the light of circumstances now?

22. How many of your organization's employee representatives have attended union-sponsored industrial relations courses over the last year? The previous year? The year before that? What are your answers in respect of managers attending management-sponsored industrial relations courses over the same period? Having reflected on your responses, what action, if any, is indicated? When?

23. In view of the effect of industrial relations policy and practice on every aspect of the organization's activity, what action do you propose to take now to ensure that all concerned are fully trained/developed to handle industrial relations issues at the appropriate level? What action could/should you take in the medium term? The longer term? And how will you ensure that what you plan to happen does indeed happen?

14 Interviewing

Your skill at interviewing people has a direct impact on both your professional reputation and the reputation of the organization you represent. Every successful interview, whether it is concerned with selection, discipline, appraisal, termination or more general fact-finding, is underpinned by effective preparation. Planning of both what you want to achieve and how it can be achieved is vital.

Introduction

1. What proportion, in percentage terms, of your job is spent interviewing for any purpose?

   - How much of your working life is devoted to:
     - Choosing people for jobs? (Selection)
     - Discussing task-related issues? (Job performance)
     - Dealing with their grievances? (Grievance)
     - Discussing their overall job performance with them? (Appraisal)
     - Handling issues of personal conduct at work? (Discipline)
     - Helping them to clarify their problems and make their own decisions? (Counselling)
     - Establishing why they have resigned? (Exit/termination)
     - Any other conversations with a purpose?

2. How important is being able to interview effectively to you *personally*? To what extent does your professional reputation hinge on your skill as an interviewer?

   - What possible action does your answer indicate?

3. How much time do you spend on preparing for particular interviews. Is it enough in your view?

4. How many articles/books on interviewing have you read in the past twelve months?

   — What effect has this reading had on your interviewing performance?

5. How much training in interviewing skills have you undergone in the past five years? Would any booster training be useful now?

6. How often do you discuss your interviewing performance with colleagues? Is that often enough?

   — How often do you invite a colleague to sit in with you on a particular interview (for instance, during selection) to review your performance? When was the last time you filled this role for someone else?

7. How much has your interviewing style changed in the last five years?

   — How has it changed?

8. To what extent do you feel your personal values affect your interviewing style? Just how far should they?

9. If you were to pinpoint one particular personal skill as being crucial to effective interviewing, what would it be?

   — What other personal skills are appropriate for interviewing purposes?
   — To what extent do you believe you possess these personal skills?
   — What action do your answers to these questions indicate?

10. Just how far do you consider yourself to be a good judge of people?

    — In what major ways do you believe you could improve your judgement of people?

11. To what extent does the law affect your interviewing style and the questions you ask?

    — If you are not absolutely sure, what action is indicated?

12. How important is it, in your view, to follow up the interview decisions you make?

    — To what extent do you follow them up?
    — What have you learned from any follow up?
    — How has the learning modified your approach subsequently?

13. What features of your present interviewing performance would you like to improve?

Purpose

14. What is the purpose of the interview?

    - To get information?
      - To assess depth/extent of knowledge/skills/attitudes?
      - To decide suitability for a particular occupation/traineeship?
    - To give information?
      - To help the individual consider available options and make a choice?
      - To help the individual to help himself/herself?
    - To enhance your reputation as a caring/helpful/concerned individual/department/organization?
    - Or what?

15. What do you want/hope to achieve?

16. What does the individual want/hope to achieve?

17. What *should* be achieved? Who should decide?

18. In view of the possible purposes, is an interview the best way? The only way? The right way?

19. What evidence have you from past experience which may have a bearing on the present situation?

20. In relation to selection interviews for instance, have you considered using:

    - Trainability tests?
    - Other vocational assessment procedures?

21. Is an interview really appropriate? Are you sure?

Information

22. What information do you need before the interview?

    - Do you have it?
      - If so, have you studied it?
      - If not, how could a lack affect the outcome?
    - Should the interview be postponed until you do have the necessary information?

Mental preparation

23. Are you prepared mentally for the interview?

- Will you devote *all* your attention to it?
- What changes/modifications to your present approach should be introduced this time?
- What relationship should you establish?
- Are you *really* prepared to listen?
- What types of question will you use to achieve the purpose(s) of the interview?
- How much talking should you do/should the individual do?
- Will you suspend judgement/avoid jumping to conclusions?

Physical preparation

24. Are facilities for the interview appropriate?

    - Temperature?
    - Lighting?
    - Appropriate seating?
    - Privacy?
    - No interruptions?

Timing

25. Have you agreed a specific time for the interview? Do you intend to stick to it? If not, why?
    Remember: lateness may be perceived as discourtesy or disinterest.

The interview itself

26. What structure should the interview take? Which elements of those shown in Figure 14.1 require particular attention?

Results

27. Has the interview achieved its purpose(s)? How do you know?

    - Are you happy?
    - Is the individual happy?
    - Was mutual understanding achieved?
    - Was there a practical/constructive/positive outcome?

28. What has been learned this time which will be of benefit for the future?

29. In what other ways will you ensure that any future interview is not damaging, either to your reputation, the reputation of the organization you represent, or the individual's future?

Welcome
Put at ease
Clarify/agree the purpose/scope
Outline/agree sequence

Getting information	**Giving information**	**Clarifying options**
Keep purpose in mind	Keep purpose in mind	Keep purpose in mind
Maintain attitude of patient neutrality	Outline prospects and opportunities	Maintain attitude of patient neutrality
Encourage individual to talk	Clarify personal responsibility	Avoid imposing own standards/criticizing
Guide discussion unobtrusively	Ensure understanding	Listen actively
Draw out information/ facts/opinions		Use the 'reflection' technique
Ask questions sensitively		'Wait out' pauses
Listen to what is said		Prompt consideration of *all* opinions
Listen between the lines		Allow individual to make own choice
Don't talk too much (20:80?)		
Encourage mutual understanding		

Parting
Be positive
Be courteous
Indicate/agree proposed action

Figure 14.1:   The structure of an interview

15 Introducing new employees

New recruits left to fend for themselves in finding out what they need to know are more likely to seek new pastures during their initial period of employment. This is known as the 'induction crisis'. Its impact may be eased by implementing systematic induction procedures for all new-comers to the organization.

1. How do you rate the quality of introduction received by new employees to your organization?

2. Is it as effective as you would like? To what extent may the following factors be indicative of a shortfall in the process?

Background indicators

Staff turnover

3. What are the rates of staff turnover by different categories (age, department, function, etc.) for new employees?

    – What is the new employee survival index?
    – Is this figure acceptable? By what criteria?

Faulty work

4. What are the rates of scrap, rework, waste? Are these and other indicators of efficiency (and effectiveness) examined regularly in relation to new employees? Are these indicators acted on? Are you sure?

The learning curve

5. From a different perspective: how long does it take for new employees in various categories to become integrated into the organ-

ization? To reach an acceptable level of performance? Is the time taken to become fully experienced acceptable?

Health and safety

6. What is the accident frequency rate for new employees? How does the new employee sickness and absenteeism rate compare with that for longer-serving employees?

7. Have the causes behind these figures been considered in detail?

Management responsibility

8. Do members of management recognize the importance of effective induction procedures? If not, why? What should be done to rectify the situation? When? By whom?

9. Who has overall responsibility for effective induction in your organization? Specific responsibility? What role should the immediate supervisor of a new employee play in induction? Who else is involved in ensuring that the new employee gains a positive impression of the organization during the first few days/weeks of employment?

   − Should the responsibility be written into every supervisor/manager's job description?

Introducing new employees: the practical implications

Operating a formal programme

10. If the answers to any of the above questions indicate a shortfall in approach, has the possibility of introducing/developing a formal induction programme been considered?

11. Are there sufficient new employees at any one time to mount a formal programme?

    − If so, how long should it last?
    − When should it be held?
      • Immediately on joining?
      • Or at a later date?
      • Have the implications of holding it later been fully considered?
    − Where should it be held?
      • Is the environment really suitable for the purpose?

12. Have the questions to which new employees will probably want answers been considered in detail? Is it accepted that the following basic questions underpin any induction programme?

    − What does the organization expect of me?

    – What can I expect from the organization?
    – Where do I fit in?

13. Which of the topics in Figure 15.1, and others not mentioned there, should be included?

    – Has the proposed programme content really been thought through?
    – How have the priorities for including particular topics been set? For instance, should a session on handling techniques be included in view of the considerable proportion of accidents, nationally, attributable to this cause?
    – Will the programme structure recognize the new employees as adults? Will sufficient time be made available for questions after each session?

14. Who should cover what topics?

    – Will a senior manager introduce the programme to emphasize the importance put on it by management?
    – Are the proposed speakers competent?
    – Will back-up speakers be held in readiness in case of illness etc?

15. What aids to learning should be included in the programme?

    – What visual aids will be used? Will these aids support the image of the organization you wish to project?
    – What printed material will be distributed? Does it present a progressive view of the organization? Is it suitably packaged? How does it relate to material already passed to the new employee on engagement?

16. What evaluation/follow-up procedures should there be to ensure on-going effectiveness?

    – Who should be involved?
    – What would be the most effective way of evaluating the worth of the programme? Against what time-scale?

17. Who should be responsible for implementing, developing and controlling such a formal programme?

Individual programmes

18. If there are insufficient new starters to mount formal programmes, do individual supervisors/managers induct their new staff effectively? How do you know?

19. Have all supervisors/managers undergone training in:

    – The importance of effective induction?
    – How to induct new starters?
    – The topics which should be covered?

The organization	The employee: personal rights, responsibilities and benefits

Background
Development
Products/processes/services
Markets
Locations
Number of employees
Organization
Mission
The future
 	
Geographical layout
Departments
Services
Facilities
Car parking
 	
Policies
Personnel
Industrial relations
Training and development
Health and safety
Communications
Data protection
Others critical to your
   organization
 	
Rules, regulations, procedures
Works/office rules
Disciplinary procedure
Grievance procedure
Check off
Notification of changes in personal
   data
Protection of organization's
   assets
Safeguarding of information
	Rights
	Wage/salary system
	– payment
	– additional payments
	   • bonuses
	   • differentials
	– incentives
	– deductions
	– loans
	– savings schemes
	– rights during sickness
	Pension arrangements
	Long-service awards
	Protective clothing
	Consultation
	Equality of opportunities
	Other rights under the law
	Further education/training
	
	Responsibilities
	Sickness
	– self-certification
	– notification
	– further certification
	Hours
	– clocking
	– overtime
	– weekend working
	– shift arrangements
	– flexitime
	– lateness
	Health, safety, fire prevention
	– personal responsibilities
	– fire drills
	– evacuation procedures
	– good housekeeping
	– special hazards

Figure 15.1   Topics relevant to an induction programme

The organization	The employee: personal rights, responsibilities and benefits

Receiving division/department
What it makes
Service it provides
Technical terms
Organization structure
Employee representation
  – safety
  – union
  – other
Relationships
Consultation arrangements
Standards
Particular hazards
	Benefits
	Holidays
	  – bank, annual
	  – relation to length of service
	Services
	  – first aid, medical
	  – private health insurance
	  – cafeteria, restaurant
	Sports and social activities
	  – clubs, societies
	Preferential purchases
	  – inside organization, in
	    locality

Figure 15.1 *concluded*

20. When did they receive their training? What booster training may be needed now?

21. Has the introduction of a standard 'induction checklist' (see Figure 15.1 for possible topics) been considered to ensure uniformity of approach? (If not, what action is indicated? When? By whom? Could the layout shown in Figure 15.2 be useful?

Name: Department		Date joined:	
Topic	Item covered (✔)	Date	By Name Title
1. 2. 3. etc.			

Figure 15.2   **Example of a layout for an induction checklist**

Follow up

22. Whether the induction is formal or informal, what follow-up should be implemented?

    – Do you recognize that the impact of any initial induction may be

lost if 'on-the-job' training practices are not of comparable quality?
 — Are those experienced staff involved in on-the-job training fully trained themselves for the role? Are you sure?

23. Has the idea of appointing individual mentors for new employees been considered for the first few weeks (or months) of employment?

Review

24. When was the last time employees with six to nine months service were asked for their views on their introduction to the organization? Were the comments acted on? Is it time the exercise was carried out again? If the question has never been asked, what does this indicate about the probable quality of the introduction?

16 Job descriptions

Job descriptions which concentrate on the results expected of job holders have a number of uses. Besides clarifying expectations, they provide a basis for both job evaluation procedures and staff appraisal programmes, as well as helping to identify training needs. A standard managerial job description, applicable to all supervisors and managers in your organization, may also be helpful in establishing general managerial responsibilities, regardless of technical specialization.

1. Do the descriptions emphasize the purpose of the jobs in your organization?

2. Are they 'ends' oriented rather than 'means' oriented?

3. If the job descriptions do not focus on major end results, what should be done? When? By whom?

4. Do they accurately indicate the dimensions of individual jobs including:
    - Role and place of the job in the organization?
    - Numbers and categories of people reporting to the job holder?
    - The job holder's immediate superior?
    - A broad indication of the scope and purpose of the job?
    - The duties and responsibilities involved?
    - The relative working importance of each activity?
    - The controls which have been built into the description?
    - The limits of authority
    - The working relationships necessary for effective job performance?
      • With people inside the organization?
      • With people outside the organization?

5. Do the descriptions highlight the essential characteristics of the environment in which the jobs operate? Are they agreed between each

Job Description Form

Job description reference no. ....

Date of preparation ....

1. Job Title	
2. Responsible to: (job title of immmediate supervisor)	
3. Responsible for: (total number of staff for whom res- ponsible; also job titles of immediate subordinates)	
4. Scope and purpose of job: (brief overall statement indicating why the job exists)	

5.   Duties and responsibilities:
5.1 Manager's 'job core' responsibilities, if
    applicable
5.2 'Technical' duties and responsibilities
    indicating the relative importance of
    activities and the limits of authority	

6. Relationships: (job titles of those people with whom the job holder must liaise in order to perform the job effectively) (i) Internal (inside the organization) (ii) External (outside the organization)	

7. Appointed by ....
(immediate superior)

Job title .... Date ....

8. Approved by ....
(immediate superior's superior)

Job title .... Date ....

9. Distribution (as a minimum those indicated in numbers 1,6,7,8,
and 9)

Figure 16.1   Example of a job description form

PLAN	Compile	Reduce	Counsel
Analyse	Conduct	Replace	Delegate
Ascertain	Contribute	Select	Develop
Assign	Co-ordinate	Solve	Encourage
Audit	Create	Specify	Help
Calculate	Decide	Strengthen	Instruct
Contribute	Delegate	Supply	Strengthen
Decide	Deploy	Support	Support
Design	Determine	Utilize	Train
Determine	Develop		Utilize
Develop	Direct	**CONTROL**	
Devise	Distribute	Appraise	**COMMUNICATE**
Direct	Establish	Authorize	Advise
Estimate	Execute	Check	Coach
Examine	Expedite	Compress	Collaborate
Forecast	Implement	Co-ordinate	Co-operate
Foresee	Improve	Correct	Confer
Formulate	Increase	Direct	Consult
Initiate	Install	Enforce	Contribute
Investigate	Interpret	Ensure	Counsel
Originate	Introduce	Evaluate	Deliver
Prepare	Maintain	Examine	Demonstrate
Prescribe	Maximize	Facilitate	Disseminate
Propose	Minimize	Govern	Explain
Review	Modify	Guide	Inform
Schedule	Obtain	Lessen	Instruct
Study	Operate	Limit	Liaise
Supply	Optimize	Minimize	Negotiate
Survey	Organize	Monitor	Participate
	Perform	Prevent	Prepare
ACT	Prescribe	Reduce	Prescribe
Achieve	Process	Regulate	Recommend
Administer	Procure	Review	Record
Adopt	Produce	Supervise	Report
Advance	Promote		Request
Allocate	Prompt	**MOTIVATE**	Suggest
Approve	Provide	Advise	Transmit
Assist	Purchase	Assist	Write
Carry out	Receive	Coach	
Classify	Record	Co-operate	

Figure 16.2 Useful action verbs for the preparation of job descriptions

job holder and his/her immediate superior?

6. What is the procedure for the preparation of job descriptions in your organization?

   – Are job holders asked first to prepare their own job descriptions?
   – Are they subsequently modified/amended as necessary in consultation with the job holder's immediate boss?
   – Who else is involved in the preparation of the descriptions? Should they be?
   – Who receives copies of each finalized job description?
     • The job holder?
     • The immediate boss?
     • His/her immediate boss?
     • Those elsewhere within the organization with whom the job holder must liaise in order to perform effectively?
   – If any of the above are excluded, why? What action does your answer indicate? Who should take it? When?

7. Are the job descriptions in your organization:

   – Accurate?
   – Clear?
   – Balanced?
   – Up to date?
   – Flexible?

   How do you know? Would a new employee fully understand his/her job by reading the job description?

8. Is there a system by which job descriptions are regularly reviewed/ updated? If so, how often do the reviews take place? In particular, are the descriptions reviewed when

   – The organization structure changes?
   – The job content changes?
   – The job holder changes?
   – Inaccuracies are highlighted?

9. Whose responsibility is the review?

10. How much does it cost?

11. How much more might it cost if it is not done?

Management 'job core' description

To the extent that all management jobs have a common element, do you accept that the following are an integral part of your own managerial responsibility, whatever your specialist function?

1. *Personnel*

   - To have the final say in selecting staff for your department?
   - To see that the responsibilities and authorities of your staff are clearly laid down and understood
   - To ensure that they have sufficient authorities for their responsibilities?
   - To ensure optimum utilization of staff in meeting corporate objectives?
   - To see that your staff are trained to fit them for their work and to develop them for increased responsibility?
   - To set standards of performance and attainment for your staff, and impartially to judge them against these standards?
   - To appraise formally and review periodically the performance of your subordinates with them?

2. *Communications*

   - To ensure that your subordinates are kept informed on matters which affect them?
   - To deal with complaints and grievances from your staff without delay?
   - To ensure that your own senior manager is informed on all matters which affect him/her?
   - In particular to ensure his/her prior approval before:
     - Changing the organization structure of your department?
     - Appointing additional staff or terminating employment?
     - Exceeding any approved budget?

3. *Industrial Relations*

   - To promote and maintain constructive relationships on all industrial relations matters?

4. *Planning*

   - To spend time regularly on planning your job and to consult with other departments affected before decisions are taken?

5. *Procedures*

   - To ensure that you and your staff follow approved corporate rules and procedures (e.g. standing orders, expositions, procedural agreements, etc.) in the execution of your duties?

6. *Control*

   - To limit your own immediate staff to a number you can effectively control and co-ordinate?

   - To delegate as appropriate without relinquishing:
     - Any part of your accountability?
     - Your overall responsibility for results?

7. *Legal Obligations*

   - To ensure that all the current legal obligations of the organization towards its employees are effectively discharged for those people within your own area of authority?

8. *Improvement*

   - To keep yourself informed on matters related to the work of your department and to make improvements in cost and any other item which will contribute to overall productivity?

9. *Protection of corporate assets*

   - To protect all corporate assets under your control against loss, waste or misuse through negligence or dishonesty?

Are all the above points either:

- Written into the job description for every manager in your organization?
- Or, issued separately as a definition of general managerial responsibilities applicable at all supervisor/management levels in the organization?

If neither, what should be done? By whom? When?

17   Listening

To listen to, and not merely to hear, what customers, colleagues and other staff members say is a vital skill. It is easy to avoid listening whether with your mind, or body, or both. To attend psychologically and physically involves real effort: but it is worthwhile.

Preliminary diagnosis

1. To what extent would you agree that your ability to listen effectively has a central impact on your job performance? On relationships at home? On contacts elsewhere? . . . and, perhaps most importantly, on you as a person?

2. How many hours formal training in listening skills have you undertaken as an adult?

    − What does you answer suggest about the likely level of your skill in this respect?

3. When was the last time you read an article or book on the subject of listening?

    − What impact did your reading have on your skills as a listener? How do you know?

4. How would you currently rate your skill at asking questions? At listening effectively to the answers your questions generate (rather than merely hearing them)? Remember: asking questions and listening to the answers represent different sides of the same coin. Rate each skill on a scale from 1 (lowest) to 100 (highest): See the grid overleaf.

5. How would those closest to you respond to the previous question? How would your colleagues respond? Your acquaintances?

    − Would the responses differ?

Self-assessment

Asking questions	Listening

— How would you account for any differences between their responses? Or similarities? Between their responses and yours?

Proposed action

6. How far do your answers to all the previous questions suggest that you could develop/extend your listening skills?

   — If your answer is 'not at all', are you sure that your responses have been accurate?
   — Are you fully aware of the many elements which contribute to a genuine ability to listen?
     • If not, what action is indicated forthwith?
     • If so, which particular elements will you concentrate on? Which of those illustrated in Figure 17.1 would repay particular attention?

7. Now review your proposed actions. What other action is necessary to ensure your good intentions are implemented sucessfully? And monitored periodically? (How will you check your progress?)

8. What are the development implications of these questions for every other manager in your organization? For other employees?

   — Should every supervisor/management training programme conducted within your organization emphasize the crucial necessity for effective listening at every level? How can you establish the need? And then meet that need?

9. Over what time-scale would any action be appropriate?

10. What are you actually going to do, both personally and on behalf of your organization, on this topic during the rest of this week? Next week? And thereafter?

Some contributory elements	Current skill level low/moderate/high	Action?	Help needed from …	Time frame (action completed by)	Criteria for success
Physical attending (Listening with your body) – Staying relatively relaxed – Maintaining reasonable eye contact – Looking interested in what is being said – Keeping still (avoiding fidgeting) – Facing the speaker					
Psychological attending (Listening with your mind) – Remaining neutral (keeping an open mind; not pre-judging) – Avoiding the mental (and verbal) 'yes, but …' – Not interrupting in other ways (e.g. answering your own questions) – Not reacting to emotional words – Listening for the theme in what is said, not just the 'facts' – Listening 'between the lines to the speaker's tone of voice – Weighing the evidence (evaluating content rather than how it is said) – Interpreting the speaker's non-verbal signals sensitively – Asking questions to ensure understanding – Not avoiding 'difficult' topics – Concentrating (resisting distractions)					

Figure 17.1 Developing your listening skills: an action plan

18 Making changes at work

It is tempting to believe that others will recognize and readily accept changes to established working practices — the advantages are self-evident, to you at least. Nevertheless, the successful introduction of changes at work depends on detailed planning and on consultation with everyone likely to be affected.

The proposed change

1. What is the precise nature of the change?

   - Why is it necessary?
   - What is wrong with what happens now?
   - How can the change be justified?

2. Compared with the present situation, what will be the advantage of the change? From whose point of view?

   - What will be the benefits?
     - For others? For you?
   - What other positive spin-offs might also be achieved?

3. What are the short/medium/long-term objectives you wish to accomplish?

   - Have you specified the success criteria in measurable terms?
     - Quality: How well?
     - Quantity: How much?
     - Cost: At what price?
     - Time: How soon?

4. When, specifically, would you prefer the change to take place? Over what time-scale?

   - Why at that time? Over that period?

    — What could happen if people do not co-operate, particularly as a tive(s)?
- Are you sure you are not trying to push the change through too quickly?
- Will the groundwork have been completed effectively?
- Will people be ready for the change when it happens?

5. Have you considered the possible disadvantages fully?

    — What industrial relations issues may be involved?
- What may have been offered in exchange for acceptance of the change?

    — What degree of contingency planning will be necessary? How much could it cost if things go wrong?

    — How far could the total costs of the change escalate, if unchecked?

    — What degree of risk is involved compared with the intended return? Is that acceptable?

    — What could happen if people do not co-operate, particularly as a result of poor communication?

    — In brief, have you given sufficient thought to these aspects? And, in particular, to the 'people' element?

6. What training will be required before, and during, the change?

    — Will the need for training be accepted? By all concerned?
    — What type of training is involved? Initial/booster/retraining?
    — Can it be provided internally? Or will external resources be necessary?
    — How much will it cost?

7. Do your objectives require revision in the light of your answers to these questions?

    — Would a lesser change be appropriate? More realistic? More acceptable?

Consulting those affected

8. Why should people accept the change?

    — Have you considered the consequences of the proposal *fully* from their point of view?
    — What is in it for them? Is this really sufficient to gain acceptance?

9. What, specifically, can you do to ensure that everyone understands the proposal?

    — Will you provide all those concerned with full background information?
    — Will you present the proposal as something less than a universal truth?

10. Will the proposed change be considered with them?

    – Will you consult *all* those who will be affected?
      • If not, why not? Can you justify keeping people in the dark? Are you sure?

11. If you propose to 'sell' the change to them, how far may the proposal pose a real threat, both individually and collectively?

    – Do you recognize that this may be the key issue?
    – How do you propose to deal with these perceived threats?
    – Who are the opinion leaders?
      • What will be the best strategy for convincing them?
    – Have you considered how easily such a propaganda sale might backfire on you?

12. Is the climate right to involve people fully in deciding the particular parameters of the change?

    – Do you accept that there is a close relationship between involvement and subsequent commitment?
    – Are you prepared for criticism of your own preferred approach to the change?
    – Are you sufficiently open-minded to heed suggestions and incorporate them in the proposal as appropriate?
    – Are you clear about your own motives in proposing the change?
      • What do you want to get out of it, personally?
      • What will others see you as wanting to get out of it?

13. What effect has the consultation process had on your original objectives? Do they need further modification?

Introducing the change

14. Once agreement has been reached on introducing the change, how will it be implemented?

    – What resources will be involved? Will these be sufficient?
    – What constraints will apply? Are they recognized by all concerned?
    – Are the contingency plans ready? Could they be brought into effect immediately, if necessary?
    – How will progress towards the target be monitored?

15. Do all concerned know what part they are to play in the change?

    – Does everyone know who will do what, why, where, when and how to implement the change?

16. What existing communication lines can be used? What new ones will need to be set up?

    – Are individual authorities and responsibilities clearly under-
      stood?
    – Are interim reporting procedures required?
    – Should a steering group be set up?
      • What should the membership be?
      • How often should the group meet?
      • For how long should it meet?

17. How will the new situation be stabilized?

    – For how long should it be monitored? Who should decide? In
      consultation with who else?
    – How easy would it be for the previous situation to reassert itself?
      What can be done to prevent this?

Follow-up

18. Has the situation improved?

    – How much better is it now? From whose point of view?
    – Have you sought the views of all those involved?
      • How do they really feel?
    – Have your objectives been achieved?
    – What positive spin-offs have there been?
    – What other unintended results has the change produced?

19. Did you approach the change in the most effective way?

    – What have you learned during the planning, execution and
      monitoring stages of the change for next time?
      • About yourself?
      • About others?

20. Was there appropriate emphasis on the human repercussions of the
    change, and not merely on the technical details?

    – Were the human consequences foreseen?

21. As somebody once said: 'There is no such thing as a technical change
    without a social effect.' What have been the social effects of this
    particular change? If they have not been wholly positive, what more
    needs to be done? When? By whom?

19   Managing stress

Stress is what happens to people when they believe they must cope but are not sure they can. Those who are suffering from stress may react to the symptoms in different ways although once on the downward spiral many people find it increasingly difficult to combat stress. Stress is no respecter of persons; a senior manager may suffer in the same way as a junior staff member.

We all have our own personal stress threshold which can be crossed at any time. Often the point of transition is not even recognized. Identifying your own stressors will enable you to plan and implement appropriate action.

Analysing your personal stress factors

Within yourself

1. To what extent do you worry about your work?

2. Are you happy in your job? Or are minor issues assuming a major significance at the moment?

3. To what extent do you believe your personality matches your job?

Within your job

4. Just how far does your job involve unscheduled interruptions over which you have little control?

   – How unpredictable is your work schedule? For this week? For this month? For this year?

5. What control 'time span' applies to your job? How soon can you be called to account for the decisions you make?

6. If you were to make a mistake, how serious would it be? What would be the repercussions for you personally? For your job? For other people?

   - Are people's health and safety in danger from the decisions you make?
   - Could their view of themselves be under threat from your decisions? Are they being made to feel inadequate?
   - Would any mistake make you feel inadequate?

7. Do you work irregular hours? Shift work? A disruptive pattern of work? Or in the evenings? Is your work itself dangerous?

The interface between home and work

8. To what extent do you take work home with you? Occasionally? Or regularly?

9. Can you switch off when you leave work?

   - Do you think about work at home? Or about home at work? To what extent in either case?
   - Can you think about your home at work? Do you? Should you?
   - Just how far might you be torn between home and work? Does any conflict make you feel guilty?

Changes in circumstances

10. Have you changed your job recently? Or taken on new responsibilities? Or even been involved in an important business readjustment (for example a merger or reorganization)?

11. Have there been any significant changes in your relationships with colleagues in the recent past? With more senior management? With other staff?

12. What changes, if any, have there been in your personal relationship with those close to you? Is this causing any 'problems' currently?

    - Have any comments been made about your moods? Approachability? About not doing things which need to be done? About your unwillingness or inability to make decisions? About being 'wrapped up' in yourself? Or about your lack of concentration?

13. Have you had to readjust to changed domestic circumstances within the past year?

    - Retirement of someone close to you?
    - Children leaving home?
    - Becoming a grandparent?
    - Divorce or separation?
    - Someone close returning to work or changing employment?
    - Moving home?

     – Suffering a bereavement?
     – Having an addition to the family?

14. Just how far are you worried about your personal finances?

     – Have you taken on any major financial responsibilities recently?
     – Have your financial circumstances changed in any other way in the past few months? How? Is it bothering you?

15. Do you have any worries currently about your health or that of any people close to you?

     – Have you noticed any minor changes recently in your own condition (for instance, headaches) when you are under pressure?
     – Are you overweight? Or even underweight?
     – Do you smoke or drink too much? Or depend on tablets to keep you going through the day?
     – Do you suffer from any longer-term health problems which may be aggravated by your 'worries'?

16. Do your answers to any of these questions suggest that stress may be a more significant part of your life than it should be?

17. To what extent would you like to do something positive about the situation? If not, could this be part of the problem? Or do you believe the pay-off might not be worth the effort? How sure can you be?

Remember: Activity is not necessarily action!

Coping with stress

18. What action could you take to control your life more effectively? To reduce your current stress reactions?

19. Which of the following possibilities may be particularly appropriate for you?

Making decisions

20. Are your work and domestic decisions thought through effectively?

     – Are you sufficiently systematic in your decision making?
     – What are your work goals currently? Your domestic goals?
     – Do you review the alternative courses of action open to you before deciding what to do? Or do you rationalize your actions after the event?
     – Have you got your priorities right?

- Would it be worth reviewing your 'must do', 'should do' and 'could do' priorities? Both at work and at home?
- Do your priorities accurately reflect current commitments?
- When you do achieve success do you feel a sense of pride?

Managing your time

21. How well do you manage your time currently?

    - Do you tend to put off the important things which need to be done? Do you procrastinate and do the unimportant but interesting things first?
    - Do you give yourself sufficient time to think? Are you sure?
    - How often do you have difficulties in meeting deadlines? In doing other things you have promised to do at home?
    - Are you spending too much time on detail at work? And squandering time at home?
    - Are you dealing with the most important and pressing issues first? In both environments?

22. Would it be worth preparing a realistic 'to do' list for action in the next seven days?

    - How does the list compare with your answers to the previous question? What action, if any, does your answer suggest?
    - Does the list show how you are proposing to break out of your own personal stress cycle?
    - Are there any items on the 'to do' list which involve helping other people control/reduce their own stress levels? Should there be?
    - How will you monitor progress against the lists you prepare in the future? Will you actually do so? Are you sure?

Your personal values

23. What are the most important things to you in your life? The most important relationships?

    - How often do you tend to forget your answers?
    - Just how important are the relationships to you?
    - What are your true priorities?

24. In view of your answers to these questions, is your perspective on both work and home realistic? Is the balance right for you? For those close to you? Are you putting all your eggs in one basket?

25. What more could you do to redress the balance? Even if you are coping reasonably well with stress at the moment, are you doing all you can to prevent it happening? Are you sure?

Preventing stress

26. How well do you know yourself?

    − Do you know what is likely to cause you undue pressure?
    − Are you aware when you are under pressure from different sources?
      • Particular individuals?
      • Particular work situations?
      • Particular domestic situations?
    − Is your initial reaction fight? Or flight? What can you do to become more assertive?
    − In TA terms, are you comfortable in your preferred stance in different situations? Would you like to change? How? Would it help you to cope better with any stress?

27. How much exercise do you take? Is that enough?

    − What more could you do to improve your physical health?
    − What more could you do to think positively? To think about your good qualities and achievements?
    − Are you aware that such action will help to prevent stress?

28. Do you maintain a sensible and balanced diet? Do you eat healthily? How do you know?

    − In general terms, are you looking after yourself?

29. What is your favourite method of relaxing? What other methods do you use?

    − Is it possible that you are mistaking inactivity for relaxation?
    − Do you sleep too much? Or not enough?
    − Does your self-view allow you to try seemingly novel approaches to relaxation?
    − How much do you know about techniques such as meditation and yoga?

30. Do you have a few close friends? Or a wide circle of acquaintances?

    − Can you really talk problems through with these people?
    − Or are your problems being 'bottled up'?

31. What actions do your answers to the last five questions suggest? Are you genuinely prepared to think through your responses? And do something positive about the situation?

32. Can you justify inaction? Are you sure? To what extent could your response be a rationalization?

33. Where will you go from here? What feelings have these questions prompted in you?

34. Are you encouraged to be proactive, to respond purposefully? Or will your stance be merely reactive?

35. Having answered these questions are you proposing to take a greater control of your life? Or to allow your stress to control it?

36. What are you really saying about yourself? Do you respect the answer?

20 Managing your time

Time is the most valuable resource at your disposal. It is also absolute. The time you have spent reading these words can never be relived; the moment has gone forever.

Making good use of your time requires a positive act of will, a self-discipline in planning the passing hours. The following questions have been designed to help you 'fine tune' your time usage.

Preliminary diagnosis

1. Are you managing your time as effectively as you might? Currently? Long term? At work? Elsewhere? Do you plan your life? Or does it have a tendency to plan you?

2. To what extent would you agree that any of the following situations could apply to you:

    - Missing deadlines?
    - Putting off things which you ought to do?
    - Spending too long on telephone calls you didn't start?
    - Having insufficient time to think?
    - Being unsure where your time goes?
    - Achieving less than you think your efforts deserve?
    - Feeling you have to say 'yes' to people?
    - Dealing personally with too many work crises?
    - Attempting to achieve perfection in tasks rather than excellence, and achieving neither?
    - Waiting for meetings which start late?
    - Indulging in lengthy evening 'naps'?
    - Failing to keep your promises on domestic tasks?
    - Arriving home late because of 'pressure of work'?
    - Thinking too much about work problems at home?
    - Thinking too much about home problems at work?
    - Spending insufficient time with your family?
    - Forgetting birthdays/anniversaries/other special dates?

- Spending too much time travelling?
- Regarding travelling time as 'dead' time?

3. Does the figure '168' mean anything to you? Or '8760'? Should these numbers mean anything?

4. Is time important to you? As it is the only absolute (irreversible) resource at your disposal, what are you planning to do in the next 365 days to extend your use of this time? To achieve more than you have to date?

5. What will you do in the next 24 hours? The next 168 (a week)? In the following 700+ (a month)? And in the 8760 hours which make up the next year from today?

	Self		Others	
	Initiated	Controlled/Monitored	Initiated	Controlled/Monitored
At Work				
Meetings				
With one person				
With small group				
With large group				
Telephone calls				
Started ⎫ work				
Received ⎭				
Started ⎫ non-work				
Received ⎭				
Dictation				
Report writing				
Reading				
Correspondence				
Professional update				
Thinking alone				
Travelling				
Other (specify):				

Figure 20.1   Current time investment   (%)

At Home

Telephone calls
  Started ⎫
         ⎬ work
  Received ⎭
  Started ⎫
         ⎬ non-work
  Received ⎭

Writing
  Work originated
  Other

Thinking alone

Reading
  Work originated
  Professional update
  Other (specify):

Entertaining/being
entertained

Watching TV/video

Listening to radio/
records/tapes

Other leisure activities
(specify):

Keeping fit

Sleeping

Other (specify):

Figure 20.1 *concluded*

Current time investment

6. How do you spend your time? What activities take up most of your time? What take up the remainder?

   − Can you locate, and subsequently quantify in percentage terms, your relative time investment using Figure 20.1
   − If you cannot, what are you doing with your time? Should you start to log your time now so that you can establish what you are doing? Over the next week? Over the next month? A longer period?

7. What seems to be the primary emphasis of the time investment you make now? Just how much of your time is self-initiated and self-monitored? How much is initiated and controlled by others?

8. Can you locate your relative time investment on the quadrant shown in Figure 20.2? (Your response will be 'clusters' of your responses to Figure 20.1.)

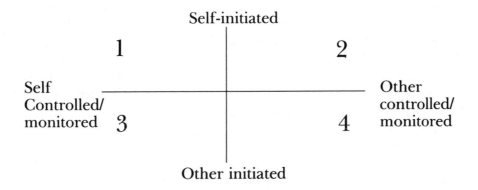

Figure 20.2   Quadrant: current time investment

9. It is probable that a majority of your time spent at work may be located in quadrant 4. It is now worth reflecting on how you could make additional space for yourself (expanding the time spent in quadrant 1)?

   − In this respect what is your answer in relation to your time at home? And elsewhere?

10. Just how much of your total time investment is spent effectively (doing the right things) rather than merely efficiently (doing things right)? Can you locate the proportions of efficient and effective time on the quadrant shown in Figure 20.3?

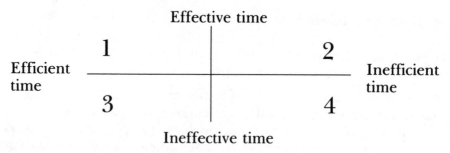

Figure 20.3   Quadrant: effective/efficient time investment

11. Are you the prime initiator/controller of your effective time invest-
    ment? Or is it initiated/controlled by others? At work? At home?
    Elsewhere? What is your answer on your efficient time investment in
    the same three environments?

12. If you were to conduct a SWOT (Strengths, Weaknesses, Opportun-
    ities, Threats) analysis today of your total time investment, what
    would be your strengths? (Using your time both effectively and effi-
    ciently represents a strength. Such strength allows you to exploit
    time which would otherwise be wasted; it certainly represents an
    opportunity to achieve more. Using time ineffectively, or ineffi-
    ciently, or both, represents a weakness which itself could constitute a
    threat, both now and in the future). What would be your relative
    weaknesses? What specifically is your current position on time plan-
    ning, usage and control?

    Can you locate your answers in Figure 20.4?

    – What do your answers suggest about ways in which you could use
      your strengths to further exploit opportunities? And the ways in
      which your relative weaknesses could constitute a threat to you if
      not dealt with positively? At work? At home? Elsewhere?
    – How do your answers compare with your current time invest-
      ment?

13. Whatever the results of your analysis, are you prepared to act to
    increase the proportion of self-initiated/controlled *effective* time
    usage? Or will you allow yourself the 'privilege' of paralysis-by-
    analysis? Will you act? Or react?

14. Having now considered the 'what?' and 'so what?' of managing your
    time effectively, will you accept the challenge? And deal purposefully
    with the last question of the trio: 'now what?'.

An improvement strategy

15. Are you now in a position to prioritize, more effectively, your current
    commitments both at, and from, home and work, using the time
    investment matrix shown in Figure 20.5?

Key area	(Please tick (✔)			
	Strength	Weakness	Opportunity	Threat

Doing the right things:
effective time investment

   1.

   2.

   3.

   4.

   5.

   6.

   7.

   8.

   9.

10.

Doing things right:
efficient time investment

   1.

Figure 20.4   Current time investment: a SWOT analysis

2.

3.

4.

5.

6.

7.

8.

9.

10.

NOTE: The identification of strengths indicates opportunities for the future: building on current strengths creates future opportunities. The identification of current weaknesses on the other hand creates the opportunity for rectification in the future. If the opportunity is declined however, the weaknesses could well represent an increasing threat.

Personal notes arising from the SWOT analysis:

Date completed ....

Figure 20.4   *concluded*

Degree of urgency

	Now (most urgent)	Soon (urgent)	Sometime (less urgent)
Must (most Important)	1.	2.	3.
Should (important)	2.	3.	4.
Could (less important)	3.	4.	5.

Degree of importance

Figure 20.5   Time investment matrix

16. Reviewing each of the items you have located in the various cells which constitute your time investment matrix, are you absolutely sure that the achievement of each item is feasible? And suitable? And also acceptable? (Remember: identifying the relative feasibility, suitability and acceptability of the priorities you have identified is just as critical to success as identifying relative importance and urgency.) Some questions which may help to determine the impact of these three critical dimensions are shown in Figure 20.6.

Feasibility	Is your proposed action realistic? Is it achievable? With or without help? What obstacles could prevent success? Can these obstacles be removed, with effort? What amount and quality of help will be necessary? Is it available now? Could the situation change? How will you accommodate any changes? At work? At home?
Suitability	Will achievement assist/promote personal productivity at work? If not, why have you included this item as a priority? Would it be worth considering both the direct *and* indirect impact of the item on your future productivity? Will achievement assist domestic harmony? Again, what will be the impact, both direct and indirect?
Acceptability	Does your proposed action meet with your own personal approval? If not, could it be that you are procrastinating? That you believe any 'problem' will solve itself, given time? That you are too busy in any event? Or that the degree of personal risk is unacceptable? Will your proposed action meet with domestic approval? If not, do priorities require renegotiation? Will the action meet with corporate approval? If not, might the degree of risk be unacceptable? Again, do priorities require renegotiation?

Figure 20.6 Your proposed actions: three critical dimensions

In assessing the feasibility, suitability and acceptability of your judgement you may care to remember the words of St Francis of Assisi: 'Grant me the courage to change those things which can and should be changed, the serenity to accept those things which cannot be changed . . . and the wisdom to know the difference.'

17. Reassessing now your answers to the personal SWOT analysis in question 12, what could you change in yourself to extend your own personal time-effectiveness in achieving your priorities? Which of

the possibilities shown in Figure 20.7, amongst others, should you consider in detail now?

Factor	(Please tick (✔))						Details of action to be taken
	Degree of urgency			Degree of importance			
	Now	Soon	Sometime	Must	Should	Could	
Controlling effect of personal stress on time usage							
Extending personal assertiveness (saying 'no' and meaning it)							
Modifying your availability							
Improving reading skill							
Using 'dead' time more effectively							
Extending your power of decision-making							
Delegating more effectively							
Extending thinking time							
Developing relationships							
Other (specify):							

Figure 20.7   Extending personal competence

18. Can the points you have included in Figure 20.7 now be added to your time-investment matrix (Figure 20.5)?

19. What in total are you committing yourself to do? Over the next week? The next month? A longer period?
    − How specifically will you ensure that your intentions (both plans and their monitoring) will be actioned effectively?
    − What else do you need to do to ensure success?
    − Will this checklist constitute a working document over the coming weeks? Or will it be quietly dispatched into limbo?

20. Are you ready, genuinely, to get started in a positive manner on improving your time-management skills? And having started, how specifically will you keep going? Do you propose to consolidate any benefits arising from this commitment? What can you do to keep the impetus going?

21 Occupational health

Advice on suitability for employment, the provision of a casualty service, and diagnosis of health hazards, all contribute to an effective occupational health service. Nevertheless, to ensure success, such provision must be supported by full training in the implementation of its objectives for all employees.

Background

1. Is there someone in your organization who has overall specific responsibility for occupational health?

    — If not, would it be advisable to consider such an appointment in order to safeguard the organization's position in relation to the Health and Safety at Work Act and other relevant legislation?
    — If so, when was this person appointed? Is he or she a qualified practitioner? To whom does he or she report? Is the appointment full-time or part-time? What are the objectives of the appointment? If a formal job description is not in use, what is the justification? Does the position carry sufficient 'weight' to ensure operational efficiency?

2. Do the objectives of the appointment include the following provisions:

    — Advice on medical suitability for particular jobs?
    — Treatment for individual employees injured at work?
    — Diagnosis of possible health hazards caused by the work itself and/or the working environment to ensure protection of individuals against these hazards?

3. Is an acceptable occupational health service based on these points in current operation? How many staff are employed? Is that number sufficient to provide such a service? Are you sure?

Advice

Employment

4. Is a medical examination an integral part of your organization's selection procedure?

 − If so, is it conducted by the organization's own staff? By a qualified medical practitioner? Or by a nurse?

 By a doctor

 • Does the doctor judge general medical suitability for employment? Or for particular occupations?
 • If the latter (and particularly if the appointment is part-time), is he/she really in a position to judge the suitability of individual candidates' physical condition for particular occupations?
 • What consultation takes place between the doctor, the personnel department and the receiving department before a final decision is made? Is that sufficient?

 By a nurse

 • Is the nurse judging medical suitability within her/his own sphere of competence?
 • Is suitability really judged? Or is the job primarily one of recording facts about the individual (height, weight, etc.)?
 • If a questionnaire is used to provide basic data (on previous medical history for instance) does the individual concerned sign it as being a true record? If not, why not?
 − Is the best possible use made of the doctor(s)/nurse(s) employed in relation to health appraisal for employment? For instance, if nursing staff were more fully involved in appraisal, would this allow the doctor(s) more time for job/environment studies?
 − Could the existing system of pre-employment health checks be improved to reduce time and cost? Would it be possible to streamline procedures by identifying particular physical conditions contra-indicative of suitability for specific occupations? Would the approach shown in Figure 21.1 be useful?

5. Are full and accurate records kept of all candidates who have been medically examined prior to appointment? For how long are these records kept? Is that long enough?

6. Is particular care given to recording the reasons for medical unsuitability? Would these records stand close scrutiny by an official body?

Disablement/Rehabilitation

7. Are records kept of jobs which are particularly suitable for disabled

Physical condition	Contra-indicative of employment involving
Respiratory	Dust, fumes, extremes of heat and cold
Epilepsy	Machinery, heights, etc.
Renal	Extremes of heat and cold
Back trouble	Lifting of weights, prolonged standing
Alimentary	Excessive shift work, irregular meals, excessive fatigue
Cardiovascular	Heights, overtime, heavy work, prolonged sitting, keyboard operation
Dermatitis	Dust, oil, liquids, food preparation and service, likelihood of stress
Sight*/Hearing/Nerves	Machinery, heights, confined spaces
Diabetes	Irregular meals, irregular patterns of severe physical activity
Pregnancy	Exposure to radiation
Muscular problems (e.g. tenosynovitis)	Keyboard operation

*For instance, what is your organization's policy regarding the employment of candidates with monocular vision? Or particular psychological predispositions?

Figure 21.1 Examples of physical conditions which are contra-indicative to particular occupational environments

persons? Is contact with rehabilitation specialists maintained?

8. If employees have been absent due to sickness for more than a specified time, are they medically examined on their return to work?

9. Is there a procedure in operation to deal with employees who request transfer on medical grounds? If not, should there be?

Treatment

10. Is an efficient casualty service provided for employees who suffer accidents at work?

11. Are all employees aware of the correct course of action to take if they suffer an accident at work? Are supervisors? Is the point emphasized during induction?

12. Does the organization meet statutory requirements regarding the

provision of qualified first-aiders? And first-aid equipment? Are you sure? Would it be worth checking just what the position is now?

13. How many qualified first-aiders have been certificated for the first time during the last twelve months? Re-certificated? How many are under training now?

14. Who is responsible for ensuring that the statutory requirement regarding notification of accidents is fulfilled? Who is responsible for ensuring that the accident book is kept fully up to date? Where is it kept? When was it last checked?

15. Are occupational health staff (first-aiders, nurses(s), etc.) aware of particular accident risks? Are they fully prepared to take any necessary action?

Diagnosis of health hazards

16. What efforts are made to diagnose possible health hazards caused by the jobs themselves or by the work environment? Is sufficient emphasis put on this preventative aspect of occupational health?

17. For instance, are studies of lighting, heating, ventilation, noise, etc. carried out periodically? And particularly when new processes, machinery, etc. are introduced?

18. What particularly hazardous operations are carried out in your organization?

    − Are relevant employees issued with protective equipment (e.g. ear muffs, protective eye wear, face masks, gloves, spats, etc.)?
      • In fact, has a check been made recently of all the protective equipment issued?
      • Is it used? Are employees fully aware of their own responsibilities to use this equipment correctly? Are supervisors? Are all those involved suitably trained? What are the current needs for booster training.
      • Is the use of appropriate protective equipment written into terms/conditions of employment?
    − What toxic substances are used currently within the organization?
      • Who is responsible for keeping an up-to-date register of such substances?
      • Are all employees whose work involves these substances aware of the hazards?
      • Are they suitably trained? Are you absolutely sure? What booster training may be necessary?

19. How does the absence rate among executive staff compare with that for the remainder of the organization's staff?

- In fact, what problems are currently being caused by executive absences due to sickness?
- What proportion of such absence may be stress-related? What action is taken now to help executives to practise effective coping strategies? What further impact could training play in emphasizing preventive action against the impact of undue stress at work?
- What action is suggested by your answers to these questions? How soon should such action be taken? Over what time-scale?

20. Are periodic health checks of executive staff carried out?

- If not, should the advisability of introducing such checks be considered?
  - Would it be worth finding out more about the services provided by private health insurance bodies?
- If not, is the agreement to undergo a regular (say annual) check written into all individual contracts at executive level?
  - What is the position on confidentiality between medical practitioner and 'patient'? And between medical practitioner and the organization as an employer?
  - Have the particularly sensitive potential problems surrounding this situation been fully recognized?

21. What contingency plans exist for dealing with longer-term sickness absence of individual executives?

- If none, should there be? Who should prepare them?

22. What was the absence rate for non-executive staff in the last quarter? In the last financial year? Is the figure rising or falling? Or is it static?

- What proportion of absences are the result of accidents at work?
- For example, how many days were lost in each of the last four quarters as a result of incorrect lifting/handling?
- What are the implications of your responses for future training activity? What could you do? What should you do? Over what time-scale?

Overseas postings/appointments

23. Are pre-appointment medical check-ups carried out for all staff posted overseas? If not, should their introduction be considered?

24. Are the current, and potential, inoculation needs of staff who travel overseas reviewed regularly?

Further action

25. If the previous questions on the possible application of an occupa-

tional health service in your organization indicate any shortfall in approach, what should be done about it? By whom? In consultation with whom?

- What should be the scope of such a service (particularly in the light of current legislation)?
- What are the particular needs of your organization?
- Is the scope and purpose of the service an integral part of your written health and safety policy (itself a statutory obligation)?
- Do job descriptions for medical/nursing staff exist? What revision and updating may be necessary?
- What advice/assistance/information should be sought from specialist organizations in the medical and occupational health fields?

26. Finally, no occupational health service can operate truly effectively unless everybody involved is trained to support its objectives. Is such training carried out in your organization? During induction? Subsequently? Is the training fully supportive of current objectives? Are you sure?

22 Performance appraisal

Performance appraisal can be defined as periodic, formal (i.e. written) evaluation of an employee's job performance which may serve a variety of purposes. Whilst there are nearly 30 appraisal methods to choose from, it should be understood that the final choice will communicate the value structure (the culture) of an organization. The utility of an appraisal programme, its purpose, its form, operation and reception are all issues which reflect organizational values.

Background considerations

1. What do the words 'performance appraisal' mean in your organization?

    - To top management?
    - To you?
    - To supervisors and managers at different levels?
    - To everyone else?

2. To what extent might the views differ? When was the last time a check was made?

3. Could anyone in your organization have made the following comments on performance appraisal?

    - It isn't needed: the good people are like the cream – they always rise to the top
    - It's just a lot of form-filling. Nothing ever happens
    - Doesn't it mean that annual get-together for the anointed?
    - Nothing to do with me
    - Going on the occasional course
    - Talking to the boss about what he thinks I haven't done
    - Just another on-cost
    - Yes, we ought to have some
    - I ask for courses but nothing's ever happened

- You'll get on anyway if the managing director likes you
- It's a good idea but they don't know how to go about it
- It's something for the top people only – not the likes of you and me
- A farce, a complete farce!
- I spend far too much time on it and then haven't got enough for my real job
- A waste of time
- I won't ever get promoted, I'm too valuable where I am
- Appraisal? It's a joke!

4. How important is it for everyone in your organization to be absolutely clear about the meaning of performance appraisal and their own personal rights and responsibilities in relation to it? Are the aims of appraisal fully understood? Are you absolutely sure?

5. Should an evaluation of what happens now be conducted as a first step towards more effective performance appraisal?

6. If ever such an evaluation should take place, will the following issues be considered?

Aims

7. What are the aims or purposes of performance appraisal in your organization? Do they include:

    - Helping individuals to improve and extend their job performance?
    - Identifying current training needs?
    - Helping to prepare people for possible promotion by identifying longer-term development needs?
    - Ensuring that sufficient suitable people are available at all levels to meet the organization's management succession needs in the foreseeable future?

    If not, what *are* the aims of performance appraisal in your organization? Whatever they may be, are equality of opportunity and positive encouragement of self-development regarded as basic principles? Are the principles honoured and carried through into practice, by all concerned? If not, why not?

8. Taking the aims you have identified, are they too diffuse? Are there too many? Are they realistic? Do they relate effectively to one another? Are they achievable? Are they achieved now? . . . How do you know?

9. Do the aims form part of a policy statement on performance appraisal?

    - Does everyone have a copy of this statement?
    - Is the personal responsibility of all supervisors and managers for

helping their own staff to develop themselves clearly specified? Is it also written into every supervisory/management job description?

- Are managers in no doubt that discharging this responsibility effectively is critical to their own personal success in the organization?

10. Is the policy derived from, and co-ordinated with, corporate business plans? If not, what does this imply about the effectiveness of your organization's approach?

11. Does the policy have the full approval and agreement of top management? If unions are involved, were they consulted and their agreement gained? If there is no policy statement, what should be done? By whom? How quickly?

The programme itself

12. Does the programme work?

- How do you know?
  - How does it compare with the approach used elsewhere in your industry? Nationally?
  - If it does not compare favourably, why not? What should be done?
  - When was the last time an evaluation exercise was carried out? With what result?
  - Is the time ripe to carry out such an exercise again now?

13. How is performance appraised? How does the system operate?

- Is performance assessed against pre-set objectives?
  - Are targets/standards of performance agreed for the review period? And subsequently assessed? By whom in the first instance? Is self-appraisal operated formally? If not, how can its absence be justified?
- Or is performance assessed in a more general way?
  - If so, just how subjective is it? Is it really fair to those being appraised? For instance, if personal qualities are rated, is the behaviour critical to the job? If not, why is it rated?
  - Are the ratings made by different managers comparable? How can you be sure? What possible action does your answer indicate?
- Does the system meet its aims? Does the documentation reflect the aims of the system? Are you sure? How do you know?

14. Are the shortcomings of a general approach to appraisal recognized fully?

- Is the procedure used in your organization open to criticism?
- Is it truly supportive of effective management action? Are you sure?

— If not, what action is indicated?

15. Are all staff, at all levels, appraised? Is the programme primarily concerned with existing managers, potential managers, or both?

   — If not both, why not? What is the justification? Does it genuinely hold water?
   — If so, how is a 'potential manager' defined? If the definition does not include all non-managerial employees, why not?

16. How often are staff appraised?

   — If it is more infrequently than once a year, why? What is the justification? Again, is that reasonable?
   — Or is it seen merely as a once-a-year activity without any follow-up in the intervening period?
   — Who is responsible for conducting the appraisal? If it is not the individual's immediate superior, why not?

17. Does everyone know exactly what their rights and responsibilities are in relation to the appraisal programme?

   — Do they know what is expected of them? Are you absolutely sure?
   — Do people believe in it? Do they want to make it work or do they endure it? How do you know?

Individual involvement

18. Is each individual appraised:
   — Fully involved in the procedure?
   — Asked for comments on his/her performance, development wishes and career intentions on the appraisal form? Or, alternatively, on a 'self appraisal' preparatory-form?
   — Shown his/her supervisor's written appraisal?
   — Given the opportunity to comment further on this appraisal? On the form? At the interview, if there is one? Or both?
   — Shown the comments of his/her senior manager?
   — Given a copy of the form when finally completed, if requested?

   If not, is the programme as 'open' as it should be?

19. If the individual is not fully involved in the ways outlined above, why not? What is the justification for conducting the exercise in confidence? How can it be fair to all concerned?

   — How can people believe in it? Or make it work?
   — Is the time ripe for review?

Appraisal interviews

20. Are appraisal interviews an integral part of the programme?

- If not, why not? How can such an absence be justified?
- If so, are all supervisors and managers fully trained and competent to discharge this particular responsibility? Are you absolutely
sure?
    - For example is training in appraisal interviewing given to *all*
    newly-appointed supervisors and managers? In coaching and
    counselling techniques? *Before* they are expected to carry out
    the interviews? If not, why not? If so, what booster training
    may be necessary now?
    - How effective are the appraisal interviews in particular depart-
    ments now? Are some better than others? Why are they
    better?
    - What action does your answer suggest?

21. To re-emphasise the point, are all those concerned in appraising
staff fully trained for their role?

    - What further training in appraisal interviewing and other
    appraisal-related techniques may be required?
    - When was the last time an audit of appraisal training needs was
    carried out?
        - With what result?
        - Should it be carried out again now?
        - Who should conduct it?

Assessment of potential

22. Is the individual's potential assessed as an additional part of the
overall procedure? If so, how is potential assessed?

    - On past performance?
    - Personality factors?
    - A combination of the two?
    - Or what?

23. Are the particular problems associated with this aspect of assessment
recognized? By all concerned? Are you sure?

    - Is potential considered in a subjective long-term way involving a
    broad prediction of latent talent? Of ultimate job level? Or is it
    specific in terms of shorter term promotability (e.g. 'now', 'in one
    year', etc.)?

24. Are the assessments of potential valid? How do you know? What
evidence is there that past assessments have been accurate?

    - For instance, are all those individuals rated as having high poten-
    tial, or being immediately promotable (say) three years ago, still
    with the organization? Is the organization helping them positively
    to realize their potential? What are these people doing now? If a
    marked proportion has since left, what does this infer about the
    quality of this aspect of development practices in your organiza-
    tion?

25. Who makes the assessment of potential?

    − The individual's immediate manager?
    − The senior manager?
    − Personnel/training staff?
    − A combination of the above people?
    − Someone else?
    − Are they competent to make such an assessment?
      • Are you sure?
      • Again, what evidence is there currently to show that the assessments made are valid?

26. Is the individual concerned informed of what his or her potential/promotability is considered to be?

    − What is your justification for this approach?
    − Is it fair to the individual?

27. Are meetings an effective way to discuss an individual's potential/promotability? Have alternative, perhaps more objective, ways of doing so been considered?

    − For instance, what use does your organization make of assessment centres in assessing potential?
    − Could their use be introduced or extended?

Follow-up

28. What actually happens to the completed appraisal forms?

    − Who keeps them? For how long? Are they genuinely regarded as working documents? Or are they merely additional paperwork to be filed?
    − If each appraising manager does not have at least a summary of the results, why not? How can action be taken subsequently?

29. Is there an internal appeals procedure for those not happy with their assessment?

    − Does it work?
    − How often is it used? What does your answer suggest about the programme's worth?
    − If no appeals procedure is operated, what should be done? When? By whom?

30. Is effective action taken on the recommendations made in individuals' appraisals? How do you know?

    − What control mechanisms exist to ensure that the recommendations are actioned as appropriate? Do these mechanisms work? Are you sure?

31. Are individual development needs fulfilled using a wide variety of

approaches and not merely off-the-job training courses?

- Do supervisors and managers recognize that on-the-job development invariably makes a much more significant contribution to
  success?

32. Which of the following on-the-job development activities play a
    positive role *now* across departments in your organization?

    - Coaching and guidance?
    - Job rotation/secondment?
    - Special assignments/working party membership/projects?
    - Planned delegation?

    How do you know?

33. What other possible development activities not mentioned here
    could be introduced? For instance, would it be worth setting up
    'training quality circles' with particular groups of managers to extend
    awareness of development issues?

34. And what benefits are built into the system for the manager who is
    both conscientious and effective in appraising his or her staff? Are
    they sufficient? Against what criteria?

Overall evaluation

35. If one aim of your organization's programme is to identify training
    needs, does it actually do so?

    - What training needs (both current and developmental) have been
      fulfilled directly as a result of identification through the appraisal
      programme in the past year? Are you happy with the answer?
    - Is the programme really fulfilling this aim?
    - What specific responsibility do individual supervisors and
      managers carry for taking action on the training needs of their
      own departments?
      - Are they proactive in meeting these needs?
      - Do they take the initiative or wait to be prodded by the training
        department?
      - Or do they abdicate altogether?
    - Do supervisors and managers genuinely recognize that one of
      their prime tasks is to help their people develop?
    - Just how effective are your organization's supervisors and
      managers in this respect? Is that effective enough?
    - What action does your answer indicate?

36. If another aim is to provide for management succession by promot-
    ing internally rather than appointing externally wherever possible, is
    this aim met?

    - Does your organization operate an effective search/placement
      system (i.e. 'in-house' recruitment/selection?)

111

- If so, do the appraisal results form an integral part of the system?
- Is the system operated willingly by line management?
  - If indispensability is used as a reason why a particular individual cannot be released for promotion elsewhere in the organization, is a time limit (say three months) imposed? If not, how many people may be languishing because they are too good to let go?
- Does the system work?
  - What is the current ratio between internal and external appointments? Has this ratio risen/fallen/remained static over the past five years?
  - What action, if any, does your answer indicate?

37. What (other) aims does your organization's programme have? Should similar questions be asked in relation to these aims?

    - On efficiency? Are things done right?
    - On effectiveness? Are the right things done?
    - On contribution to corporate plans?
    - On acceptability?

    In broad terms are these aims met?

38. In view of your answers to these questions, does it appear that your organization is operating effectively in this area? Or is there a short-fall between what happens and what you consider to be the best practice?

39. Could part of the problem lie in the resources devoted to the function?

    - Are they merely adequate? Or even inadequate?
    - In either case what could be done to
      - Resource the function more effectively?
      - Encourage a more proactive approach on the part of all concerned?

40. What else could be done to ensure that every member of staff makes an optimum contribution to corporate success?

23　Personnel profiles

There are a number of well-known methods of specifying the ideal candidate for a particular vacancy. Perhaps the most commonly used is the one originally put forward by Professor Alec Rodger and known as the 'Seven point plan'. The headings used here, and the supporting questions, are based on this method.

A personnel profile (or person specification) can be derived from the job description and a knowledge of the physical and social conditions in which the job is performed. Not all ten headings are necessarily relevant for every profile: it is wiser to concentrate on a smaller number of critical attributes.

The personnel profile performs an important role in the selection process: its use as a yardstick against which candidates are assessed should not be underestimated.

What are the attributes required in a successful candidate for a vacancy?

1. **First impressions**

   What sort of first impression should the successful candidate give? In terms of appearance? Dress? Cleanliness? Voice? Manner? Social experience? Poise?

2. **Knowledge, skills and experience**

   What does the job require in terms of:

   - General education and examinations passed? How important is fluency in languages or other specific academic attainments?
   - Specific training (e.g. trade apprenticeship, national certificate, specific courses on knowledge/skill areas)?
   - Relevant experience (e.g. type of work, length and level of responsibility)?

113

3. Mental ability

How 'bright' should the successful candidate be in relation to the population as a whole? What level of analytical ability is appropriate?

4. Aptitudes

How far does the job require particular facility in:

- Understanding mechanical principles?
- Dealing with figures?
- Drawing aptitude?
- Verbal expression?
- Manipulating tools, components, etc?
- Musical or artistic talent?

5. Leisure interests and activities

How far does the job require real skill in:

- The social sphere? (Persuading, managing, understanding, helping, entertaining or being with people?)
- The practical–constructive sphere? (Manipulating, repairing or constructing things?)
- The physical active sphere? (Outdoor pursuits or those involving considerable physical effort and agility?)
- The intellectual sphere? (Solving problems requiring a scientific or logical approach?)
- Artistic expression? (In colour, design, layout?)

6. Personal qualities

What kind of role does the job involve in terms of:

- Initiative?
- Reliability or steadiness?
- Loyalty?
- Acceptability to others?
- Conformity to existing attitudes/behaviour in the department/organization?
- Decisiveness?
- Influencing others or taking the lead among them?
- Self reliance?
- Acceptance of responsibility?
- Emotional maturity?
- Perseverance?
- Readiness to learn?

7. **General background**

   Is it advisable that the successful candidate should be married or unmarried? Without dependents? Able to travel?

   - Is personal financial stability important?
   - Is a fidelity bond appropriate?

8. **Motivation and expectations**

   What levels of expectation will the job satisfy with regard to:

   - Pay/salary and fringe benefits?
   - Recognition?
   - Achievement?
   - Application of professional knowledge?
   - Career progression?

   How hard will he/she have to push himself/herself? How much energy/effort is appropriate?

9. **Health**

   What standards of general health and fitness are required? Are there any particular points concerning height, strength, special strain on limbs, vision, hearing, handedness, ability to work under particular job conditions which are important?

10. **Age**

    In view of all the previous requirements, is an age limitation (both minimum and maximum) appropriate? Is it realistic? Do you ensure that you do *not* perscribe a 25-30 year-old with 20 years' work experience?

    ---

11. Have all the above attributes required in the successful candidates been considered? Have priorities been realistically established? Has a distinction been made between essential attributes (musts) and desirable attributes (wants)? Has any possible over-prescription of essential attributes been avoided? Are you sure?

12. What measurement criteria will be used, particularly for intelligence and personality? Is a medical examination part of the selection procedure? If so, is the doctora ware of the requirements indicated in the profile? Is he/she sent a copy before the examination takes place?

13. Is the successful candidate's sex a genuine occupational qualification? What are the implications for the recruitment/selection procedure?

14. Are there any contra-indications? (Any negative attributes which would mean immediate disqualification from further consideration, for example a candidate under a driving ban applying for a job as a travelling sales representative.)

Personnel Profile

.... (Job title)

Factor	Attributes	
	Essential	Desirable
1. First impressions		
2. Knowledge, skills and experience		
3. Mental ability		
4. Aptitudes		
5. Leisure interests and activities		
6. Personal qualities		
7. General background		
8. Motivation and expectations		
9. Health		
10. Age		

Is sex a genuine occupational qualification? If so, please specify and give reason(s) ....

....

Contra indications (if any) ....

....

If applicable, minimum test results acceptable:

Intelligence
Personality
Aptitude
Other (specify)

Prepared by .... Date ....

Job description no. ....

Figure 23.1   Example of a personnel profile

24 Preparing for an appraisal

Managers tend not to prepare effectively for the appraisal discussions in which they are involved. For many staff it is the only formal occasion in the year when they can discuss matters which concern them. Evidence suggests, however, that the results of such discussions do not have the positive effect on job satisfaction which might reasonably be expected.

Reflecting before the event on what you can do to achieve more fully the aims of the appraisal discussions you conduct will help both you and your staff to derive greater job satisfaction.

Background considerations

1. What are the stated aims or purposes of appraisal in your organization?

2. To what extent do you 'massage' the formal aims towards what you think they ought to be ? If your answer is 'not at all', are you sure?

3. Do you accept that periodic review of the performance of your staff with them is an integral part of your job as a manager?

4. Are you fully committed to the process of appraisal? If not, what are you saying about your own chances of progression in the organization? And about treating your staff fairly in this respect?

5. Are you fully competent to discharge your commitment?
    -   How many days training have you undergone in relation to appraisal processes?
    -   How long ago did the most recent training take place?
    -   When was the last time you read an article or a book on the subject?
    -   What action, if any, do your answers suggest?

118

6. Are you absolutely sure you appreciate why the appraisal is to be conducted?

Preparing for the appraisal itself

7. What information do you have by which you will judge the individual's performance?

   - Is it really sufficient from your point of view?
   - Is it enough from the individual's point of view?
   - Assuming a self-review is an integral part of the procedure, have you studied the individual's response in detail?
   - If a self-review is not carried out, why not? Is the individual sufficiently involved? Is review something done genuinely with people, or merely about them?
   - Could you request a written self-review in this case?
   - Are you now truly in a position to make an objective assessment? Are you sure?

8. What actions were agreed with the individual for this appraisal period? What priorities were agreed?

9. Which parts of the job were particularly testing? In what ways?

   - Time needed?
   - Time available?
   - Personal application?
   - Ability?
   - Interpersonal skills?
   - Or what?

   Why? Was it planned? What is the individual's view?

10. Just how far was the individual's performance affected by circumstances? Did these circumstances help or hinder performance? How? To what extent?

11. What is your overall view of the individual's performance?

    - How well has the individual performed against each target?
    - How closely does your view compare with that of the individual?
      - Was more achieved than you expected? Or less? Why?
      - Which tasks were performed particularly effectively? Less effectively? Why?

12. What particular abilities has the individual utilized in performing the tasks? How could these be developed further?

    - What action could the individual take personally?
    - What joint action/commitment could be agreed?
    - What personal commitment from you may be appropriate?

119

13. What particular lack of ability may have prevented the individual from achieving success? As a result, what specific action could be taken to ensure success in the future?

    — By the individual?
    — By you?
    — By both of you jointly?

14. What, if anything, is the individual doing in relation to his or her own self-development?

    — On whose initiative?
    — What does your answer indicate about the individual's approach to the job?
    — What part should your answer play, if any, in the written appraisal? In the subsequent discussion?

15. What scope is there to develop the job? To what extent has the individual done so? How far does it seem the individual might do so in the future?

    — What action, if any, do your answers indicate? On the individual's part? On your part?

16. How often have job-related progress discussions taken place during this appraisal period? With what effect? Have the discussions been reflected in extended performance? What reference should be made to this aspect in the written appraisal?

17. Having considered the background to the appraisal in broad terms, are you now in a position to complete your detailed analysis of the individual's performance during the appraisal period? Do you recognize that the quality of your analysis will affect directly the quality of the subsequent discussion with the individual?

18. What possible tasks and priorities for the next appraisal period should be covered during the discussion?

19. How should the discussion be structured? What do you want to include? What may the individual want to discuss? What should the agenda be? Are you absolutely clear in your own mind what has to be covered? And in what order?

20. At what point will you inform the individual of the place, date and time of the appraisal discussion?

    — Will you ensure that the individual has sufficient time to prepare?
    — Is the timing favourable? For both of you? Are you sure?
    — How will you ensure that the discussion is conducted in private and that there will be absolutely no interruptions?

21. Are you sure you will allow sufficient time in your diary for the discussion?

    − Have you allowed a contingency period within the time (say half-an-hour) to ensure that the discussion is not interrupted?

22. If you have allowed less than 1½ hours in total for the discussion, are you sure you are giving both of you the best chance to succeed?

After the discussion

23. Was your planning effective? Did the discussion achieve its purpose? How do you know?

    − Are you satisfied?
    − Is the individual satisfied?
    − Was mutual understanding and commitment achieved?
    − Did the discussion have a positive outcome?
    − Have the follow-up sessions been positive?
    − If there has been no follow-up, are your responses to the first two questions in this checklist still valid?

24. What have you learned during your preparation, and the subsequent discussion, which will be of benefit to you in the future? What specific steps will you take to ensure that any learning will not be dissipated over time? What else will you do to extend your performance in this respect? When? How will you monitor your own progress?

25 Preparing for negotiation

Successful negotiation depends on detailed planning. Researching the topic, preparing the case thoroughly, accommodating likely contingencies, knowing your own strengths and relative weaknesses (and those of others involved) are all part of the process.

Applying mature personal judgement during the negotiation itself, based on previous planning, will help to ensure a successful conclusion.

Introduction

1. Do you accept that negotiation takes place whenever you are involved in a situation where the intention is to change relationships?

2. As a manager, do you recognize that you spend a considerable proportion of your time negotiating?

3. Have you ever undertaken a formal training course in negotiation? Or have you learned purely by experience?

4. If so, has the experience been cumulative? Do you consider yourself to be a successful negotiator?

5. Is there room for improvement? If so, have you ever analysed your basic approach to negotiation?

6. Are you aware that there are two basic types of negotiations – integrative (mutual interest) and distributive (I win – you lose)?

Mutual interest negotiations

7. Do you accept that:

    – The basic aim of this type of negotiation is to make sure that everybody gains something?

- This aim can only be achieved by agreement?
- Agreement itself can only result from recognition of mutual interests?
- Mutual interests can never be recognized if you are pressing for the best possible deal? A lesser percentage of a good thing is better than 100 per cent of nothing?

'I win – you lose' negotiations

8. Do you accept that:

   - This is basically a conflict bargaining approach?
   - It is concerned with the allocation of limited resources?
   - Your aim is to negotiate the best possible settlement from your own point of view?

General negotiating considerations

9. Are you aware of the differences implicit in these two types of negotiating?

   - That if either the required settlement, or the likely problems encountered in reaching it, are fundamentally different for each side, then the negotiation is highly likely to be of the 'I win – you lose' type rather than the 'mutual interest' type?

10. Do you also recognize that:

    - Both types may be encountered in the same negotiation but that your strategy and tactics will depend primarily on your recognition of which type predominates?
    - Your opponents's perception of the situation and the strategy/ tactics he/she uses are equally important?

Self-knowledge

11. Do you know yourself?

    - Have you ever assessed yourself? What action is indicated on your part?
    - What are your strengths as a negotiator? Your weaknesses? What improvement action are you taking? For instance, do you know when to stop? To forgo an advantage? Can you 'wait in haste' when there may well be a temptation to act impetuously or give in to provocation?

Knowledge of opponent

12. Are you aware of your opponent's strengths and weaknesses? Motives? Needs?

13. What does he/she want from the negotiation? Personally? For others?

Listening technique

14. Do you accept that a good negotiator is able to maintain a balance between intelligent listening and effective speaking?

15. Do you recognize that listening is as much a persuasive technique as speaking?

16. Are you a good listener? When listening do you:
    - Think ahead and anticipate reactions?
    - Weigh the evidence?
    - Think about what has been omitted and decide whether it is relevant to the negotiation?
    - Recognize the different levels at which your opponent's statements can be considered?
      - What he/she *seems* to be trying to communicate.
      - What can be inferred from the way he/she communicates and the words used.
      - What he/she conveys by the manner of approach to the subject.
    - Make every effort to observe and interpret the details of your opponent's non-verbal signals (gestures, facial expressions, movement of limbs, blinking, coughing, yawning, etc.) which can reveal emotional state?

Preparation

17. Having considered these background issues, how do you feel your preparation could be improved? Would fuller consideration of the following issues be helpful?

18. *Aims*
    - Who has instigated the forthcoming negotiation? You or someone else? Or is the negotiation periodic?
      - If you: What is your specific aim in entering this negotiation?
      - If someone else: What is his/her specific aim, if known (if not, the most probable aim)?
      - If periodic: What is the joint aim? What precedents have already been set?
      - Is it basically an 'I win – you lose' or 'mutual interest' situation?
      - If agreement is to be based on mutual interest, what is the widest possible divergence mutually acceptable.

- What will be the essential *minimum* negotiated position acceptable to you? What points will it also be preferable to achieve?

19. *Research*

   - Do you have all the necessary background information? Have you done the necessary research?

   Facts/figures
   - What do you know already?
   - What do you need to know?
   - What would you also like to know?
   - What is your opponent's position on the above questions?

   Those involved
   - Have you recognized all the interested parties to the negotiation?
   - Do you know your opponent(s)? Their strengths? Weaknesses?
   - Who would like to maintain the 'status quo'?
   - What do they really want from the negotiation?

20. *Indicated action*

   - Based on the above, what action, if any, can you take now to strengthen your position for the negotiation? How?
   - Can you use the grapevine to transmit and receive information? Or informal meetings?
   - Can you condition your opponent's reactions/expectations?
   - Can you change the timing of the negotiation, by either bringing it forward or putting it back, to better suit your own aim(s)?
   - What action, if any, might you be able to force your opponent to take to strengthen your position?

21. *Indicated restraint*

   - Is there anything you can stop doing to strengthen your position?
   - What, if anything, can you stop your opponent doing which will strengthen your position?

22. *'Rules'*

   - What 'rules' are applicable?
     - What existing agreements must be upheld?
     - Has a time limit been placed on the negotiation? By whom?
     - Alternatively, is there a natural time limit?
     - Does the time limit favour you? Or your opponent?
     - Are there any penalties involved in the negotiation (such as a penalty for bluffing or giving false information)?
     - Can many items be introduced into the negotiation simultaneously?
     - What would be the cost of a stalemate?

23. *Assumptions*

  - What assumptions have you made about the negotiation? Do you recognize them?
  - Do you accept that assumptions when taken as absolute fact can be a major obstacle to successful negotiation? That you are taking a calculated risk if you do accept assumptions as fact?
  - Have you calculated the risk?
  - Will these assumptions be tested during the negotiation?
  - What other 'hidden' assumptions may be made?
  - What assumptions is it probable/possible that your opponent has made?
    • How will this affect your thinking?
    • Are there any 'assumed' certainties?

24. *Contingencies*

  - Have you allowed for contingencies, particularly those which may originate from your opposition?

25. *Constraints*

  - Have you evaluated the main constraints to your case? Your opponent's case?
  - How will this affect your assessment of possible alternative approaches?
  - Have you considered the tactical possibilities bearing in mind:
    • Your aim?
    • The calculated strength of your negotiating position?
    • Your opponent's strength?

26. *Tactics*

  - Will your tactics be offensive or defensive? Punch or counter-punch?
  - Have you considered the various tactical approaches open to you?

  Your opponent's case

  • Will you let your opponent make his/her case first?
  • Are you ready to question his/her facts? Assumptions? Conclusions? Any ommissions/inconsistencies in the case?
  • Are you ready to amplify any weakness and use it to consolidate your own position?
  • How will you amplify such a weakness?

  Your opponent

  • If your opponent effectively maximizes the strengths (and minimizes the weaknesses) of his/her case, are you prepared to adopt the maxim 'If you can't beat the case, beat the person'?
  • If so, have you considered deprecating his/her experience, etc?

Or even exceeding your opponent's physical/mental exhaustion threshold?
- Have you really examined his/her personal weaknesses?
- Are you sure you can cope?

Your own case
- Will you go for the 'second shot'?
- How will you best indicate the benefits of your case to your opponent?
- Will you maximize the strengths of your own case whilst also maximizing the weakness of his/hers?
- Are you ready to demonstrate mastery of the details of your case?

Readiness

27. What else have you learned from previous negotiations which will help you to be more effective this time? Are you really ready for the negotiation?

26 Problem solving

Dealing with day-to-day problems skilfully is the basis of effective decision making. Such skill is not developed overnight. It is the product of much experience and trial and error. The approach taken here is based firmly on logic and illustrates a step-by-step method for analysing, and dealing with, the work problems you encounter.

Defining the problem

1. What is the nature of the problem?
   - What is the extent of the problem?
     - What is going wrong?
     - Does it concern one restricted area or does it impinge on other areas?
     - Is it generating conflict within these areas or between management in these areas?
     - What more could go wrong if nothing is done?
   - What is its significance?
     - Are there any social, political, environmental, legal or religious aspects?
     - How does the problem affect other people?
     - How does it relate to the corporate culture?
   - Is it an isolated problem or is it associated with a cluster of existing or latent problems?
     - Does the problem relate to a 'once-for-all' issue, or is it likely to recur?
     - Could its solution provide political leverage for dealing with other problems?
     - What additional opportunities might be 'opened up'?
   - Can you locate the problem on the quadrant illustrated in Figure 26.1.
   - What quadrant description appears to be most appropriate: simple/static (easiest to deal with), complex/dynamic (the hardest),

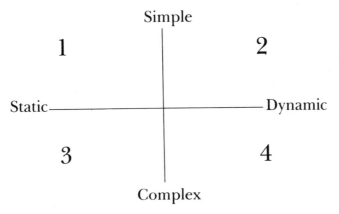

Figure 26.1 Problem location

or what? Remember: you have most time to deal with a quadrant 1 problem, and the least time to deal with one located in quadrant 4.

— What would be the cost of doing nothing?

2. What is your aim in solving the problem?
   - Can your aim be stated precisely?
     - What do you want to achieve ultimately?
     - Have you set for yourself an intended state of affairs – a target?

3. Do you recognize that the gap between the present state of affairs and the target is a problem-gap to be bridged?
   - Can you identify the various factors which constitute the obstacles to a solution? Are these factors controllable or uncontrollable? How predictable or unpredictable are they as future factors?
   - What are the chief flaws, weaknesses or deficiencies which must be put right?
   - Have you listed these critical factors (the problem dimensions)?
   - Can you rank them in order of importance?
   - Can you also 'weight' these factors? Assume for instance you have 100 points to allocate between them. (This approach – listing, ranking and then weighting the critical factors – is helpful in establishing which are the toughest issues you must deal with first and the sequence in which you should tackle them.)

4. Can you now:
   - Restate your aim?
     - Is it realistic? Practical? Achievable?
     - Is it measurable?
   - Clarify the criteria which must be met by a solution? (Cost, time, percentage changes, ratios, degree of risk, etc.)
   - Identify the problems to be overcome? In priority? Can you identify clearly your 'musts' in relation to 'wants'? (Perfection vs excellence, efficiency vs effectiveness.) Does the aim truly answer the question 'How will I know when I've got there?'

Analysing the problem

5. Who must:

    − Make the decision?
    − Be consulted?
    − Be informed?
    − Discuss the problem?
    − Translate the decision into action?

6. Have you resisted all the 'common-sense' exhortations to find out the facts first?

7. Do you remember that no one knows which facts are relevant until the problem has been defined and classified? And that until then all data is just 'raw data'?

8. Have you considered what information you need?

    − How relevant, representative, reliable and valid is the data you have now?
    − What additional data do you need? In what form?
    − Have you reviewed all the possible sources of information open to you?
      • People? Their knowledge? Their experience? (Networking)
      • Places?
      • Documents?
      • Own knowledge?
      • Own experience?

9. Have you examined and re-examined your pool of information?

    − Does it reveal that you have wrongly identified the problem or wrongly classified it?

10. Have you taken into account that:

    − Not all facts will be available?
    − Some will be too costly to obtain?
    − There may not be enough time?
    − Any search for additional information may represent only a marginal gain?
    − Compared with 'need to know' information, the 'nice to know' equivalent can prove expensive to generate? If so, have you noted and acknowledged your guesses and assumptions? Have you really accommodated the constraints on your analysis?

Generating options

11. Do you accept that developing alternative options is difficult because everyone runs the danger of seeing only one pattern − the one they are accustomed to?

12. How can you generate alternative options?

    − By reviewing other cases to search for an analogy?
    − By brainstorming the problem − suspending judgement to allow the free flow of ideas?
    − By other methods? If so, what?

Evaluating options

13. Have you generated sufficient alternatives? What are the relationships between the alternatives, if any? Are they mutually exclusive? Or can they be recombined?

14. Has each alternative been considered in turn against:

    − The criteria set (cost, time frame, etc.?)
    − Degree of risk?
        • Have the risks been weighed against expected gains?
        • What are the associated opportunities and threats?
    − Commitment over time?
        • For how long would the organization be committed by the decision? Would the decision constitute a precedent? With what implications?
        • How quickly could the decision be reversed? Could it be reversed?
    − Economy of effort?
        • Which of the possible courses of action will give the greatest results with the least effort? Are you mindful that the greatest results may require the greatest effort?
    Do not choose the easiest option too soon: it may not be the 'best'. For instance, how far does the degree of effort/commitment compare with the degree of risk, as shown in Figure 26.2.
        • What other similar comparisons may be appropriate?
        • Which option will produce the needed change with the least disturbance to the organization?
    − Legal imperatives?
        • What legal statutes must be considered? National codes of practice? Industry codes of practice? (Have internal procedures also been considered?)
        • How might they be invoked? With what effect? At what cost?
    − Timing?
        • If the problem is urgent, would a dramatic approach be best? What would be the likely repercussions of such an approach?
        • Should it be kept secret? Could such secrecy be justified? Are you sure?
        • If it is a long-term course of action (Figure 26.1, quadrant 1?), would a slow, steady start be advisable?
    − Resources?
        • Are the necessary resources currently available to carry out the plan? If not, what time-scale would be necessary to make them available?

131

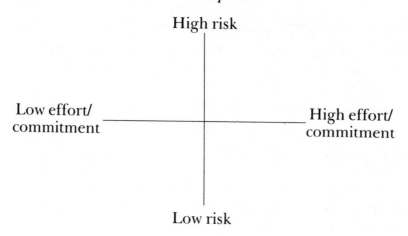

Figure 26.2   Risk/effort identification

- What would be the effect on, and of, the people involved? Their particular personalities? Attitudes? Skills? Knowledge?
- Could any vested section/department interest sabotage the plan?

Remember: it is no use solving one problem to create another. What could be the 'knock-on' effect? What new, and different, problems could be generated?

15.   Can you now decide on the 'best' (your preferred) option?

Preferred option

16.   Have you decided:

   − What action must be taken?
   − Within what time frame it will be actioned?
   − By whom?
   − Who will implement the decision?
   − When they should be informed?
   − How they should be informed?
   − Who else should be told?
   − How they should be told? (See Checklist 18)
   − What contingency plans are necessary?

17.   Have you written down the details of the plan systematically so that all concerned will know:

   − The background information to the problem?
   − The aim of the plan?
   − The operational method?
   − The administrative support?
   − The communication network?
      • Who should be informed for action? For information purposes only?

What else could/should you do to ensure the fullest understanding/commitment?

18. Have you established a control and monitoring system?
    - What checks will be needed? For how long?
    - Have the contingency plans been fully accommodated?
    - What progress reports will be needed? From whom? To whom? When?

    Are you truly ready now to put the plan into action?

Review

19. Has the solution been effective? Fully? To what extent was it necessary to reconcile variances? To implement your contingency plans? For what reasons?

20. What lessons have been learned for the future? By you? By others? What action does your answer suggest?

    Decisions often have to be made quickly and frequently the satisfactory one must be accepted in place of the ideal. These questions provide a 'hard' strategy — a stimulus to thought in the analysis of problems and in decision making from one particular perspective. They do not represent a sequence which must be slavishly worked through every time a problem arises, as shown in Figure 26.3.

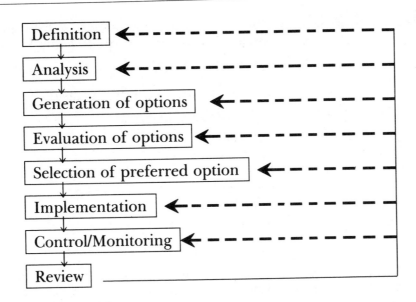

Figure 26.3 Problem solution: some pathways

Is it worth considering an alternative ('soft') strategy? If the distinction lacks meaning for you, what action may be appropriate? When?

27 Recruiting trainees

Trainees are the seedcorn which will ripen into maturity in the future. Their recruitment and selection is only the first part of a much longer training and development process.

An analysis of current recruitment sources, and their effectiveness, will provide the basis for any changes necessary.

School-leavers

Background considerations

1. How many school-leavers does your organization recruit annually? Are you in any way concerned about the quality and quantity of candidates coming forward for consideration?

2. Are analyses conducted periodically to establish trends in basic data relating to these school-leavers?

    - Numbers recruited by source?
    - Qualifications at entry?
    - Subsequent suitability for jobs for which recruited?
    - Courses of study by day release/evening classes?
    - Number of resignations?
    - Reasons for resignation?
    - Length of time employed before resignation?

3. If any of the above factors is causing concern, what is being done to improve the situation? Have the following points been considered?

4. Are academic staff (principals, headmasters, career advisers, heads of department, course tutors) fully in the picture regarding the sort of school-leavers you wish to recruit? Are you sure?

5. When was the last time a representative of your organization had contact with these staff to discuss recruitment requirements?

6. Is an effective public relations image maintained through:
    - Representation at schools and colleges?
    - Careers conventions?
    - Personal contacts?
    - Involvement in work experience programmes?

Representation at conventions

7. Could this contact be improved both quantitatively and qualitatively? If, for instance, few enquiries result from this activity, have you really evaluated the possible reasons?
    - How does your organization compare with the competition from other potential employers?
    - Schemes of training? On-the-job? Off-the-job?
    - Wages/salaries?
    - Opportunities for advancement?
    - Fringe benefits?

Personal contact with academic staff

8. When was the last time a school careers adviser was invited to visit your establishment to review personally the range of opportunities offered? Or do you feel that such advisers steer potential recruits away from the sort of environment you offer and would not be interested anyway?

9. In either case is more effort needed to establish/update the relationship? By whom? How?

10. Is it something which falls squarely within the remit of the training specialist? What about assistance from other (possibly more senior) officers of the organization?

Personal contact with relatives of potential applicants

11. What efforts are made to inform parents/guardians of potential recruits about the opportunities offered by your organization?
    - Has the possibility of holding explanatory 'open' meetings been considered? (For example, a careers convention-type exercise on-site with both potential applicants and their parents.) Could ex-student employees act as ambassadors?
    - If not, should the possibility be considered in detail? By whom?
    - What other possibilities should be considered?

Work-experience programmes

12. Is the organization positively involved in promoting work-experience programmes? How committed is the involvement? Is

every effort made to enable participants to extract maximum benefit from individual placements?

13. What percentage of placements have been converted to permanent positions? Is this percentage directly related to the organization's level of commitment to such programmes?

14. Has the organization's commitment to work experience been thoroughly evaluated? How recently? What action, if any, is indicated now?

15. In view of your answers to these questions does your organization really have the reputation among school-leavers that you believe it ought to have? If not, what action is indicated? Who should take it?

Universities/polytechnics/colleges

Policies

16. How many graduates (and graduate equivalents) have been re-cruited by your organization in the past five years? If more than a handful have been recruited, is there a positive policy concerning their recruitment, training and subsequent placement? Is this a reflection of positive human resource planning to meet future corporate staffing needs? Are you sure?

17. What has been the percentage rate of resignation in this particular category during the five-year period?

Wastage

18. Is there any discernible pattern among those who have left the organization?

    − Time with the organization?
    − Academic discipline?
    − Sponsored compared with post-course recruitment?
    − Sandwich compared with full-time?
    − Period under training before taking up first appointment?
    − Type of appointment?
    − Reason for resignation?

Employment conditions

19. Are you sure that the training, work conditions, salary, fringe bene-fits and opportunities for advancement are comparable with other organizations? When was the last time a check was made?

20. For instance, is the time spent under training, before placement, too

long? Is your organization still operating a system of 'graduate' train-eeships which may be effectively demotivating the new recruits?

Assessment techniques

21. Whatever your answers to these questions, is your organization's current approach to recruiting trainees supported by effective assessment techniques?

22. For example, to what extent are interviewers' skills appropriate now to their role? What evidence is there of recent personal development in this context? Is that sufficient?

23. Is your organization's use of psychological tests fully effective for the purpose now? Are you sure? When was an evaluation last carried out? If tests are not used, should their introduction be considered? When? By whom?

24. What other assessment techniques are used currently? Are they applied effectively? Are you sure? What additional techniques not used now should be considered for introduction in the future?

Developing recruitment and placement

25. Has the possibility of appointing line managers as 'personal counsel-lors' (mentors) been considered? If not, should it be? Who should consider it?

26. Is there a specialist member of your organization's staff, part of whose specific responsibility it is to initiate, maintain and develop effective contacts with university appointment boards? And with graduates once appointed?

27. Are you assuming that the name and image of your organization will be sufficient to attract and retain graduates of the 'right' calibre? In fact, what, specifically, are the advantages of recruiting graduates compared with recruiting school-leavers and subsequently training them?

28   Report writing

The ability to prepare a well-structured concise written report which achieves its purpose is not as widespread in organizations as might be supposed, although it can be developed relatively easily. A systematic approach, understandable to the reader, is the foundation of a good report, and can be achieved with practice.

Background considerations

1. Why are you writing this particular report?

    − Is the report really necessary?
    − Are you sure?

2. What are your objectives in writing the report?

    − Have you defined these objectives clearly?
    − Do the objectives state clearly and unambiguously what you intend to achieve?

3. Is the report your own idea? Or someone else's?

    − In either event who will read it?
    − To whom should the report be sent on completion? For action? For information?
    − Who are you really writing the report for? Why does that person matter most?

4. How will the report be used? Bearing in mind your answer to the previous question, what information should be presented graphically? Diagramatically? Pictorially?

    − How can you ensure optimum impact on the reader?

5. When should the report be presented?

    − When is the report needed?

- Will you allow a contingency period within your planning to accommodate any results of 'Murphy's law'?
- What would be the consequences of late presentation? For the organization? For you?

6. How should the report be presented?

  - Under a covering memo?
  - In person?
  - In some other way? How?

The report itself

The title

7. What is the title? Is it a short summary of the subject?

  - Does it reflect accurately the contents of the report? Are you absolutely sure?
  - What expectations might the title cause the reader to have?

The contents

8. Is there a table of contents?

Summary

9. Is there a summary? Is it clear and concise?

  - Does it contain a clear statement of your objectives? Your conclusions? And your recommendations?
  - Is it no longer than one A4 page?

Introduction

10. Does the introduction provide a frame of reference for the reader? Has it defined the background to the report? The current situation? The theme of your report? The method you have adopted for analysis?

  - Does it act as a reminder?

Headings

11. Is the text grouped under main headings?

  - Is each main heading of approximately equal importance?
  - Are the headings presented in a logical progression?
  - Do they exclude each other?
  - When considered together, do they equal the subject of the report?

Words used

12. How will the reader react to the words you have used in the report?

    − Have simple words been used? Or are they complex?
    − Are they concrete? Or abstract?
    − Have unnecessary words been included?
    − Will the reader be able to picture the words readily?
    − Have active verbs been used?
    − Have cliches and stock phrases been used too frequently?
    − Do any specialized terms require explanation? Would the inclusion of a glossary of such terms be useful?

Sentences

13. Do sentences average not more than about 20 words? And say what you mean without any ambiguities?

14. Are sentences varied in length? And suitably punctuated to help the reader understand?

Paragraphs

15. Do paragraphs have topic sentences?

16. Is each paragraph limited to a single topic? And limited in length?

17. Do the paragraphs progress naturally?

Conclusions

18. Are your conclusions drawn exclusively from the main text of the report? Are you absolutely sure?

19. Have you made any inferences which are not fully supported in the text? Have you checked?

    − Are the facts of the case clearly distinguishable from your opinions?

Recommendations

20. Are your recommendations based firmly on the conclusions? Are you absolutely sure?

21. Are the recommendations realistic? Practical? Legal?

    − Are they fully costed?
    − Are time frames clearly specified?
    − Do they relate directly to the objectives defined at the outset?
    − Are they presented in order of priority?
    − Are any constraints on action clearly identified?

Appendices

22. Have you numbered any appendices?

23. Are the appendices referred to in the main text? Are you sure? Is there any unnecessary detail in the main text which would be more effectively presented as an appendix?

Distribution

24. Has the distribution list been clearly indicated?
    − Who should *not* see the report?
    − What would be the consequences of sight by any unauthorized person?
    − What actions, if any, do your answers suggest?

25. Is there a clear definition of who is expected to take action as distinct from those who are receiving the report for information purposes only?

Presentation

26. Does the front of the report indicate clearly who originated it? And when?
    − Is the title of the report suitably emphasized? For example has it been 'boxed' and located prominently on the front page?

Quality assessment

27. In money terms, how much has it cost in total to prepare the report?
    − Your time?
    − Others' time?
    − Use of equipment?
    − Materials?

28. Was the money well spent?

29. Are you pleased with the physical presentation of the report?
    − Is the print clear?
    − Is the paper suitable?
    − Are the covers appropriate?
    − Do the pages turn easily?
    − Is the report easy to handle?
    − Will it stand usage?

30. Are you pleased with reactions to the report? Has the action taken subsequently on your recommendations justified the cost of pro-

ducing the report? Are you sure?

- If not, what does your answer say about the quality of the report? Or its need?

31. What actions, if any, do your answers to the four previous questions suggest?

32. What actions do your answers suggest to *all* the previous questions suggest? Could it be said of any report you prepare that you write to express? Or impress? . . . How do you know?

29 Self-development

To take personal responsibility for your own development requires a continuing act of will: not only to assess periodically your development needs but also to persevere in responding purposefully to these needs. Only you can decide what help, if any, you will need in achieving particular aims, and only you can decide whether your personal investment of time and effort in your own growth is paying appropriate dividends.

In any event, it may be worth noting that if you do positively plan your own development, then it is far less likely to plan you. Can you afford to be reactive, rather than proactive, in planning your own future? The following questions are designed to help you respond proactively to the needs you yourself identify.

Preliminary diagnosis

Your beliefs

1. What are the beliefs, the values, by which you lead your life? At work? At home? Elsewhere?

    — How have you come to hold these beliefs?
      What is their origin?
    — Do they mostly reflect your upbringing? Your education? Or particular people? Or some other influence? If so, which?

2. Are your beliefs consistent with one another?

    — Do any beliefs vary according to the context in which you find yourself?
    — Just how strongly do you hold them?
    — When was the last time you reviewed where you stand now?
      What action, if any, does your response suggest?

Your job

3. How are your beliefs reflected in the job you do? And in the effort

you devote to your job?

- What do your answers suggest about the work you do? And how you do it?
- Are you in the right job?

4. How would you describe your job to someone who doesn't know you?

- What specifically do you do? What is the focus of your work?
- What are your key areas of responsibility?
- Are you currently successful? By what criteria? How do you know?
- How would others describe your approach to your job? Your current success level?
- What action, if any, do your answers suggest?

5. Do you possess written terms of reference for your job (a job description)?

- If so, is the description accurate? Up to date? Focused on ends rather than means?
- If not, how do you know what your job entails? Having reflected on your answers are you happy with them?

6. What were the results of your most recent appraisal?

- What is your own immediate manager's view of your job performance?
- What development actions, if any, were agreed during the discussion? Who took the initiative in identifying any necessary actions?
- What do your answers suggest about the quality of the appraisal? And your own contribution to it?

Where are you going from here?

Your personality

7. How would you describe your personality to someone who does not know you?

- What do you believe are your strong points as a person? How do you know?
- What do you believe are your weaker points? Again, how do you know?
- What is there, specifically, about you which contributes positively to your job performance? To relationships at home? And elsewhere?

8. How would your colleagues describe your personality?

- Just how closely would such assessments match your own self-view?
- What, if any, are the critical differences in views?

    – What do these differences in view tell you about yourself?

9. How do you get on with your boss?

    – What is the basis of your assessment?

    – What could you do to extend/consolidate this relationship? What action could you take? What could your boss do? Would it be worth talking through the possibilities?

10. Generally speaking, are you assertive in your relationships with others?

    – Do others see you as assertive, rather than aggressive or submissive?

11. Do you tend towards 'type A' behaviour as a person? Or towards 'type B'? What does your answer tell you about yourself?

    – If the distinction lacks meaning for you, what action is indicated?

Your knowledge

12. How would you describe your knowledge of the job you do?

    – Are you fully informed about *all* the facts involved?

    – If not, what specifically do you not know which you should know?

       ● How could you inform yourself? How soon?

13. How would you describe your knowledge now about the job you might reasonably expect to be promoted into?

    – How could you better inform yourself? What specific action could you take?

    – For instance, how well informed are you *now* about your organization's procedural and substantive industrial relations agreements?

14. What other action could you take to extend your knowledge of the organization you represent, its culture, operations, markets, competitors and future plans?

15. What newspaper(s), trade magazines, professional journals and other similar material do you currently read?

    – Is your reading genuinely relevant to the three preceding questions?

    – Would it help to read less of more relevant material? Or to develop further your 'speed-reading' technique?

    – What action does your answer suggest?

16. Of the management/professional books you have read in the past year, which has had the most direct impact?

- What happened as a result of reading this particular book?
- If you cannot answer readily, what are you saying about your choice of reading in the last twelve months? Or your willingness to read?

Your skills

17. What professional skills do you currently possess? What additional skills will you need in the future?

   - What are you currently doing to acquire such skills?
   - How are you acquiring them? And how do you rate your progress?

18. Just how proactive are you as a learner?

   - What is your preferred style of learning?
   - What action is indicated if you are not sure?
   - What action are you currently taking to develop a more balanced learning style? Is this sufficient? Are you sure?

19. To what extent could your interpersonal skills be extended?

   - How far could your physical attending skills be improved when you are listening to what people say?
   - Could your psychological attending skills also be improved? For example, just how effective are the questions you ask during conversations and at meetings?
   - How effective are you in persuading others to do what you would like? At work? At home? Elsewhere?
   - To what extent could you extend your skill in coaching staff? Do you truly help them to help themselves?
   - Do the various types of interview you conduct invariably achieve their aims? How sensitive are you to the feelings of those around you? And just how 'political' are you? How comfortable are you with your responses?

20. Looking back over the past three months particularly, how well have you used (managed) your time? Have you extracted full advantage from the 2000+ hours involved?

   - What, specifically, have you achieved in this time?
   - How much better use could you make of your time? How could such increased effectiveness be achieved?

21. How do you currently rate your capacity to produce novel responses to day-to-day problems?

   - Just how creative are you?
   - Could your capacity be extended with effort? How?

22. How effective are you at managing the invariable stress of everyday life?

- What effort particularly do you take to reduce the impact of stress on your job performance? On your health?
- What more could you do? What should you do?

23. To what extent do you suffer undue stress when making a verbal presentation?

    - Can you identify the causes? What can you do to improve the situation?

24. What are people's reactions to the reports you prepare? Are the reactions invariably positive?

    - Have you received formal training in report preparation? If so, how long ago did it take place? If not, what can you do yourself to improve your skill?

Factor	Strength	Weakness	Opportunity	Threat

Knowing yourself

Having clear aims for
the future

- personal
- job

Relationships

- with boss
- with colleagues
- with others

Knowledge

- professional
- organizational
- industrial

Skills

- professional
- learning
- interpersonal
- time management
- creativity
- stress management
- presentation
- managing change
- reading

Figure 29.1   Personal assessment: a SWOT analysis

25. What changes to working practices have you proposed recently at work?

    - Have they been implemented? If not, why? If so, was their implementation achieved successfully?
    - How far did an assessment of your organization's culture contribute to the success of the changes? Or their failure?

A personal SWOT analysis

26. The preceding questions illustrate a few of the issues involved in personal competence at work. In broader terms how would you rate your overall skill as a manager?

    - Which elements of your managerial role do you feel would repay particular attention? Planning? Implementation? Control? Communication? Motivation? Or something else? In terms of knowledge? Or skills? Or both?

27. Can you now complete a SWOT analysis (see Figure 29.1) of your current position? Remember: a *Strength* allows you to exploit opportunities which could otherwise be wasted; a *Weakness* on the other hand could constitute a *Threat*, both now and in the future.

28. Now reflect on your SWOT assessment. What does it tell you about yourself? About your personality? Your knowledge? Your skills? The job you do?

29. What specifically are your main strengths?

    - How can you use these strengths to make more space for yourself over the coming months?

30. What specifically do you consider to be your main weaknesses, if any?

    - What could you do to reduce the impact of individual weaknesses?
    - How could you best use the space provided by your strengths? And minimize any threats?

Your plans

31. To re-emphasize questions 1 and 2, do you accept that your own personal *development* is your own personal *responsibility*? That if you do not help yourself, others are hardly likely to do so, apart from perhaps asking you to attend the odd course? And that such a request might be made at very infrequent intervals?

32. Do you also accept that whilst your own learning is your personal responsibility, you will probably need help from others to achieve

whatever targets you set yourself?

33. Are you now ready to plan, implement and monitor your own learning?

34. Can you complete the skeleton action plan, shown in Figure 29.2, indicating your proposed actions in the short term (say three months)? The medium term (up to one year)? And in the longer term?

    – What particular checklists included within these pages may be helpful in refining your proposals?

Factor	Help needed from (name(s))	Target	Achievement by (date)	Follow up/ monitoring

Short term

Medium term

Longer term

Figure 29.2 Action plan

35. Now reflect on your proposals. Are they realistic? Are they achievable with effort? And within the time-scales you have specified? Are you sure? Which people are you proposing to involve in your learning? Are they the right people? Would it be worth discussing the establishment of a self-help (co-counselling) group?

    – If this term has little or no meaning for you, would it be worth finding out more?

36. Are you genuinely now ready to get started on developing yourself? Will you be proactive in this respect? And keep the impetus going?

Or will your proposals be overtaken by seemingly more pressing matters, so encouraging a reactive stance?

37. How often will you refer to the action plan you have prepared? How often will it be replaced by a successor? When are you planning to review all the preceding questions in this checklist? Is that soon enough?

    – Do you accept that your personal development must be continual to be truly effective? And that this takes real effort? Not just good intentions?

38. What do your answers tell you about yourself? Are you happy with the answer?

30 Setting up a learning event

There are many approaches to adult learning. The following questions represent one particular method and are aimed at encouraging you to review your own approach to the training and development programmes to which you contribute.

Background considerations

You

1. Who are you?

2. What are your characteristics as a person? Your values?

3. What is your perspective on adult learning and self development?

   - What do the words 'learning' and 'development' mean to you?
   - Do you accept and treat adult learners as individuals, with individual learning needs? Are you sure? Do you accept the full implications of the question?
   - Do you adopt a 'helping' rather than a 'teaching' stance?
   - Do you positively discourage adult learners from dependence on you?
   - Do you positively discourage yourself from believing that you know best what is good for them?
   - Do you see yourself as a co-learner?
   - To what extent might there be a gap between what you think your approach to learning is (your 'espoused' view) and what it is in practice (your 'in-use' approach)?

4. What are your own learning/development needs in terms of this particular event?

5. What are you hoping to achieve personally?

151

6. What are you hoping to help the learners to achieve for themselves?

The learners

7. Who are they?

8. What are their characteristics as people? Their values? How different are they from one another?

9. What are their perspectives on learning and self-development?
    - How do they view the words 'learning' and 'self development'?
    - How do they prefer to learn?
    - Do they prefer to develop themselves? Or be 'developed'?
    - How might they be helped to develop their individual approaches to learning?

10. What are their learning/development needs?
    - How have these needs been identified?
    - Have the learners themselves been involved in the identification of these needs?
    - If not, how will you/they ensure the success of the event?

11. What do they want to get out of the event?
    - How do you know?
    - Could it change as the event progresses?

The organization

12. What are the organization's values? Its views on what should be achieved?
    - What specifically does the organization want? How will success be measured?
    - What would be the political implications of such 'success' or 'failure'?
    - How does the answer fit with your own personal values?

The psychological contract

13. Do all the stakeholders know where they stand in relation to the event? Do they appreciate the implications of what adult learning involves?

14. Has an appropriate psychological contract for the event been achieved?

The learning event

The purpose

15. In view of the above answers, what should be the purpose of the learning event? Who should decide it?

16. Is it appropriate that the purpose should be clarified before the event? Or should it be left until the event is under way? Again, who should decide? If not the learners, why not?

17. Are all concerned fully aware of the implications arising from such an approach?

18. What mix of learning aims (informing/skilling/developing) and levels of learning (memory, understanding, application, transfer) is appropriate to this particular learning event?

    − Is the truism that 'adults learn by doing, not by being told' reflected in the purpose?

19. Is the purpose justifiable? Realistic? Practical? Within the constraints which apply? . . . from everybody's point of view?

20. Will the purpose be 'owned' by the learners? Are you sure?

The design

21. In view of the purpose, what learning design is appropriate?

    − Will the learners themselves be involved in deciding the design? If not, why not?

22. What methods/approaches would be most effective in meeting the purpose?

    − In what mix?
    − If the learners are not involved in this decision, why not? Can the approach be justified? From whose point of view?

23. What is the environment within which the design will be implemented?

    − What abilities are assumed in those participating in the event?
    − Are these assumptions realistic?

24. Is the design creative? Capable of being implemented a number of times? Does it need to be?

Implementation

25. What factors should be considered in implementing the design?

    — What should be your role?
    — What should be the role of the learners?

26. Do you possess the necessary mix of interpersonal skills to implement the design? Do you have the ability to:

    — Ask the right questions to help self-discovery?
    — Listen actively without prejudging what is said?
    — Allow learners to make mistakes and take responsibility for their own learning?
    — Withstand the emotional pressure from those who may wish to be 'taught the right way'?
    — Help learners 'own' their own learning?

27. Have you the necessary conviction to persist in this approach even when feelings are running high? Are you sure you can be 'comfortable' in your persistence?

Evaluation

28. What evaluation of the learning event should there be?

    — Who should make the decision?
    — If the learners themselves are not to be involved, why not?
    — When should the broad decision be taken?

29. What methods should be used?

    — What alternatives are available?
    — Who should review them?
    — How should the different perceptions and needs of those involved be accommodated?

30. What should be evaluated?

    — The purpose of the event?
    — The design?
    — The implementation?
    — The evaluation process chosen?
    — The totality?
    — Or something else?
    — Who should decide? When?

31. What should be the order of priority? How quick must the evaluation be?

    — Why that quick?
    — What are the longer-term implications of the event?

32. When should the evaluation be carried out?

    — Continuously throughout the event?
    — At the conclusion?
    — At some other time?

33. Who should be involved in the evaluation?

    - If the learners themselves are not involved, why not?
    - Who else must be considered?

34. What other follow-up should there be?

Conclusion

35. Will those involved be fully aware of *all* their responsibilities (to themselves and others) within the context of this event?

36. Will the event reflect a mature approach to adult learning in which all concerned have the opportunity to experience significant learning through:

    - Self direction
    - Self motivation?
    - Self development?
    - Self evaluation?

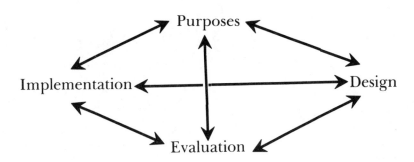

Figure 30.1   The interrelationship between the four main elements of the learning event

37. Will the event also reflect the critical interrelationship between all four main elements as shown in Figure 30.1

38. Will all learners contribute to all four elements? Will the event be truly learner-centred? Will it really be suitable for *adults*?

Some final thoughts

39. What feelings do these questions arouse in you?

    - Are you encouraged to be reactive? Or proactive?

40. Some would say that any checklist, particularly one which uses words

you may not like or appreciate, has a strictly limited usefulness. How do you feel?

41. Having considered the questions, what self development, if any, do you propose to pursue now?

42. As an adult answering this final question, what are you saying about your own approach to your own learning?

   − Are you satisfied with the answer?

31   Staff development

A prime task of any manager is to help his or her staff develop their capabilities, not only within their current jobs but also in prepapration for more senior positions. These capabilities may be extended, in most instances, more effectively in the work environment than by attendance at off-site training courses. The following checklist illustrates a variety of techniques which may be used separately or in combination. Whatever the choice in invidividual cases, however, development plans should be prepared in consultation with each person concerned: possibly during the normal appraisal discussion and periodically thereafter.

1. Do you accept that it is one of your prime management tasks to help your staff develop their job performance?

2. To what extent could the job performance of many, if not all, of your people be improved? How specific can you be? Have you considered in detail their individual strengths? Areas of competence? Areas of possible development? Are these questions considered with them? Or merely about them?

3. Do you personally devote sufficient time *now* to considering the ongoing development needs of your staff?

4. When was the last time you carried out an audit of development needs in your department? Would it be worth doing again now?

5. How do you identify the individual development needs of your people? Do you start by considering the main areas of possible development? (See Figure 31.1.)

6. Is the situation discussed, and agreement reached, with the person concerned on appropriate development targets?

   – Are the results to be achieved stated clearly?

157

Focus of action	*Targets*
Remedial	Improving particular aspects of performance which are not up to standard for whatever reason
Developmental	(a) Reinforcing personal strengths (b) Acquiring new skills and knowledge to cope with future work challenges
Creative	(a) Developing better ways of dealing with existing tasks (b) Discovering ways of dealing with new tasks

Figure 31.1   Main areas of possible development

    — Are specific time frames agreed?

7.   How often do these discussions take place with individual staff? Is that often enough?

8.   When considering the possible methods of reaching the targets, do you recognize that on-the-job development invariably makes a much more significant contribution to success than off-the-job training courses?

    — What is the balance, both qualitatively and quantitatively, between off-the-job training and on-the-job development activities in your department?
    — Are you satisfied with the answer?

9.   Which of the following development activities play a significant role in your department? Which ones could be used more? Or introduced for the first time? What is the overall balance? Is it acceptable?

Special assignments/working parties/projects

    — Would special assignments to investigate specific problems for defined periods of time add to the individual's knowledge and experience?
    — How should such assignments be monitored?

Committee assignment

    — Would such assignments broaden experience and knowledge, and increase confidence in achieving results by negotiation and discussion? How could such assignments be arranged? Could the individual deputize for you?
    — How should progress be monitored?

Coaching and guidance

- Which individuals might benefit particularly from your personal help?
- What help, specifically, is appropriate?
- What pre-planning is necessary?
- How might fruitful discussions be set up? And 'learning contracts' agreed?
- Do you possess the interpersonal skills appropriate to be an effective coach?
- What is your relationship now with the individual(s) concerned? Does a firm base for coaching exist already?
- How should progress be monitored?

Job rotation/secondment

- Would the individual benefit from broadening/updating his or her technical knowledge/experience? Supervisory/management experience?
- How critical is the need?
- Would rotation within the department meet the need? If so, when? For how long?
- If not, could secondment to another department/division be arranged? To a supplier/customer? To some outside agency? Again, when? And for how long?
- In any event, how should progress be monitored?

Study for formal qualifications

- Should the individual be encouraged to study for further technical or professional qualifications?
- What are the possibilities of encouraging the individual to join an organization-based distance learning group (e.g. Open University, Henley Distance Learning programme)?
- How close are your ties with local higher education establishments? Are you aware of the opportunities on offer?
- What monitoring is appropriate?

Membership of professional societies

- Should the individual be encouraged to participate actively in a particular professional society? To stand for office to gain wider administrative/managerial/public relations experience?
- How? When?

Planned delegation

- Which of your present responsibilities/tasks might provide a valuable learning experience for individual members of staff?
- How should these tasks be delegated? Verbally? Or in writing?
- To what sort of approach would each individual react best?

159

- Will all those concerned be made aware of the responsibilities you have delegated?
- Will you leave the individual concerned to get on with the job? Will you also delegate the right to be wrong?
- Will an attitude of 'watchful neglect' be appropriate on your part?
- When the the tasks are completed, how will you evaluate the effect of your delegation?
  - On the individual? With the individual?
  - On yourself? (See also Checklist 8)

Mentoring

- Has the possibility been considered of appointing 'mentors' (i.e. helpers) from amongst your more senior staff to assist in the development of inexperienced staff?
- Which of your more experienced staff might also be helped to develop themselves (development-by-self) by assuming the role of mentor to particular individuals (who would experience development-of-self)?
- If such a possibility has not been considered, should it be? When? Who else should be involved?
- What monitoring would be appropriate?
- If 'mentoring' is an unfamiliar term, what should you do? What will you do?

Planned self-development

- Are individuals actively involved in their own self-development?
- If not, would it be worthwhile asking everyone to conduct a written personal assessment of their own contribution to departmental efforts? And to prepare subsequently a proposed action plan (similar to that illustrated in Checklist 20) for discussion with you before implementation is agreed?
- What monitoring of self-development plans takes place currently? Should such monitoring be extended?
- What more could you do to extend the impact of self-development as a staff development tool? What should you do? What will you do? (See also checklist 29)

Off-the-job training courses

- If a training course appears to be the most (only?) effective way of meeting a particular development need, how will the most appropriate course be chosen?
  - On reputation?
  - On cost?
  - On availability?
  - Or what?
- Will the individual concerned be fully briefed before the event?

  – Will agreement be concluded on
   • Why attendance is considered appropriate?
   • What your expectations are concerning pre-course preparation? On return from the course? (See also Checklist 12)

10. What other possible development methods not mentioned above could you use to encourage a more critical self-awareness of personal performance standards amongst your staff?

  – How can you encourage them to be more proactive about their learning? How can you help them to develop their approach to on-the-job learning?

11. What action do you intend to take now? What targets do you intend to set yourself? What steps will you take to extend your commitment to helping your people develop themselves?

12. How willing are you to commit yourself to discussing progress every week with at least one member of your staff?

13. How much time will you devote each week to reviewing overall progress and formulating appropriate action plans? Half an hour? An hour? More?

14. How will you monitor your own self-imposed development targets?

32 Staff turnover

Replacing staff who have resigned can be a very expensive process. The total cost of recruiting and training a new employee may well be a substantial four-figure sum. Multiply even one thousand pounds by the number of leavers from your organization in the last twelve months: your answer is likely to show a serious, and continuing, financial haemorrhage. Minimizing avoidable turnover helps to reduce operating costs, and may be achieved by an assessment of the factors responsible before any action is taken.

1. Do you know what your organization's staff turnover has been during the past:

    − three months
    − six months } Overall and by various categories (age, sex, department, etc.)?
    − twelve months

   If not, why? If so, how was it measured?

2. Is that a reasonable measurement? What other measures could you use which are not being used now? Do they include any of the following?

    − Crude rate of labour turnover, i.e:

    $$\frac{\text{No. of employees who left in one year x 100}}{\text{Average no. employed during the same year}}$$

    − Fringe or perimeter turnover, i.e:

    $$\frac{\text{No. of engagements + no. of leavers during the past year x 100}}{\text{No. employed one year ago}}$$

    − Skill dilution index, i.e:

    $$\frac{\text{No. of skilled staff with one year or more service x 100}}{\text{No. of skilled staff employed at present}}$$

− Stability index, i.e:

$$\frac{\text{No. employed now with one year or more service x 100}}{\text{No. employed (with one year or more service) one year ago}}$$

Is the current stability index at least 80 per cent? If not, what action is indicated forthwith?

3. How much is this staff turnover costing the organization? Have you considered the true economic cost? Does your costing include the following factors:

   − Loss of leaver's skill?
   − Loss of output?
   − Recruitment and selection of replacement?
   − Training (including induction) expenses?
   − Higher scrap/wastage during training?
   − General administrative expenses?

4. How does the total cost compare with the organization's cash turnover?

5. Is the proportion steady/rising/falling? If it is rising, what action is indicated forthwith? By whom?

6. Are records kept as a basis for action? What action? By whom?

7. Are exit/termination interviews held?

   − If not, why not ?
   − If so, by whom? Line management? Immediate boss? Personnel? If the immediate boss is not involved, why?
   − When are they conducted?
   − Does objective information result?
   − How do you know? Is the information recorded from subsequent analysis? If not, why not?
   − Who is responsible for taking action on the results?
   − Is that the right person?

8. Do more people tend to leave from:

   − Particular job categories?
   − Departments?
   − Age groups?
   − Wage salary ranges?
   − From within particular travelling distances of work?
   − Are the records of terminations sufficiently detailed for accurate analyses of leavers in these categories to be conducted? And in other categories like gender? And length of service? Do the records distinguish clearly between voluntary leavers and others (caused for example by death, retirement or dismissal)?

9. Do really know who is leaving? And why?

10. Are too many good people leaving?

11. Are those that are leaving no loss?

12. Could any of the following be possible causes of the problem?

    Selection

    - When was the last time that the effectiveness of the selection procedure was checked?
    - Are there particular difficulties in filling specific jobs? Why?
    - Could the jobs be made more attractive to potential applicants?
    - How competent are those responsible for selection? Are they fully trained? If not, what should be done? When?

    Induction

    - Are new staff inducted into the organization? Formally? Or informally?
    - Is the induction effective? How do you know?
    - How competent are those responsible for induction? Are they fully trained/experienced in what is required?

    Training

    - Are new staff fully trained for their jobs? By whom? Have the trainers themselves been trained in techniques of induction?
    - Is the training effective? When was it last reviewed? By whom? With what result?
    - How do payment rates during training compare with the full trained rate?

    Supervision

    - Are supervisors fully aware of *all* their responsibilities for subordinates?
    - Have they been trained for their role? Or have they learned the ropes as they have gone along?
    - Are vacancies discussed with supervisors prior to selection?
    - Do applicants meet the supervisor for whom they would be working, before the final decision is made?
    - Does the supervisor make the final decision on who will be employed? If not, why not?
    - Is communication to and from supervision effective?

    Conditions/hours of work

    - Have the job conditions and hours of work been reviewed to assess the possible improvement/greater acceptability to employees?
    - Would it be possible to restructure jobs to provide greater interest and involvement?

Career progression

- Is an employee's performance periodically and regularly appraised?
- Does this appraisal form the basis of a positive career development structure at all levels?
- Are all employees aware that their progression depends on job performance?
- If no structure exists based on performance appraisal, could this be persuading people to take their services elsewhere?

Wage/salary structure

- Is the wage/salary structure based on job evaluation?
- If not, how can you be sure that it is equitable?
- Is it understood by all concerned?
- Is an incentive scheme in operation? If so, could it be improved? If not, should the introduction of such a scheme be considered?
- How do wages/salaries compare with those paid by other local organizations?

13. Are any of these factors capable of improvement? If so, why haven't they been acted on before?

14. Can you justify your present level of staff turnover? Do you ever have to justify it? If so, what are you doing to reduce it?

15. What positive plans have you for reducing it by x % in the next six months?

33 Succession planning

Ensuring continuity of effort in achieving organizational objectives is a perennial problem for managers at all levels. It involves planning for both the unexpected (resignations, long-term sickness, and more), and the expected (retirements). It does require considerable self-discipline to deal with what may never happen, although it is inevitable that some staff movements will occur. How you deal with both contingencies and the planned development of staff will affect your own managerial reputation.

Current situation

1. What is the present staffing situation in the department(s)/sections(s) for which you are responsible?

    — By department/section?
    — By skill level/occupational category?
    — By wage/salary grade?
    — By age distribution?
    — By gender?
    — By length of service?

2. How many staff have resigned in the past twelve months? How many have been dismissed? What is the current absence rate? Is it rising/steady/falling?

3. What does this information about the current staffing situation tell you? What is its impact now on results in your area?

4. What is the current annual cost to the organization of employing these people? Of employing you?

    — How much could be saved by making better use of the skills and knowledge of individual staff? Of your own skills and knowledge?

166

5. How much do you know about the relative strengths of your staff at all levels? Is this a sufficient basis on which to plan their future?

   – Does the performance appraisal system indicate which staff are likely to succeed in what jobs in the future?
   – Are the recommendations arising from the performance appraisal system being acted on now? Are you sure? How do you know?
     • Who needs training? Or retraining?
     • In what skills?
     • When? Over what time-scale?
   – What action do your answers suggest?

6. Which jobs in your area (other than your own) are critical to results? How easy is it for you to answer the following questions with regard to 'key jobs'?

   – Job title?
   – Current job holder?
   – Age?
   – Time in job?
   – Next job?
   – Current development plans?
   – Planned replacement?

   What are the strengths in your area? What potential problems (possible weaknesses) does your analysis suggest?

Future requirements

7. What will be the effect of the organizations's future plans on staffing levels in your department(s)/section(s)?

   – Looking forward from today, will more/less/different people and skills be needed? In a year's time? In two years' time? A longer period?
   – Which jobs, not currently vital to overall performance, could become so as a result of these changes? Who could be developed/develop themselves for these jobs? Present job holders? Or others?

Action

8. What are you doing now to ensure that future staffing needs in your area will not cause disruption? Are you genuinely planning ahead? Or are staff crises continually planning you?

9. What additional information concerning your staff do you need to generate/request from others?

   – Do you know *now* who will reach normal retiring age in the next year? The following year? The year after that?

- Are you absolutely clear about who could replace key staff in the event of accident? How ready would they be?
- Or do you believe in pitching people in at the deep end to see whether they can swim? If so, do you accept readily the responsibility for periodically removing the floating corpses?
  - What could this approach be doing to your professional reputation as a manager?
  - What could it be doing to you as a person?

10. What action are you currently taking to ensure that the fullest use is made, amongst others, of the development methods illustrated below to help individual members of your staff to prepare themselves for the future?

    - Coaching and guidance
    - Special assignments/projects/working parties
    - Committee assignments
    - Job rotation/secondment
    - Study for formal qualifications
    - Planned delegation
    - Mentoring
    - Off-the-job training courses

11. What more could you be doing now? What more could your section heads/supervisors be doing? In what ways particularly do you show by your actions that you consider 'people planning' to be fundamental to future success? Are you really doing enough?

12. For instance, what are you doing now to develop your own successor?

13. Which member of your staff would you choose to assume your own responsibilities if tomorrow, for whatever reason, you were unable to continue?

    - Why would you choose this person? Are your values showing through your answer? Or your prejudices? Are you really operating on the basis of equal opportunity for all?

14. Is this person as ready as he or she can be to do the job now?

    - If not, do you accept that you are lessening your chances of moving on if you do not adopt a proactive stance in this respect?

15. What were the results of this person's most recent appraisal?

    - What is your estimate of the individual's performance currently? How big is the gap between ideal and actual performance?
    - What specifically is the cause of this gap?
    - What development action was agreed at the most recent appraisal discussion? Is it happening? When did you last check?

16. What skills need to be developed? What additional knowledge is

needed? What attitudes still need to mature?

- What are the agreed priorities? And the time frames?
- In which context, principally, will the development take place? On-the-job? Or off-the-job?
- Can the critical needs be achieved by more committed coaching from you? By delegating new tasks? By using other methods illustrated earlier? Or by using external training courses?

17. Will you discuss these additional development proposals with the person concerned?

- Will any decisions be made jointly? If not, why not?

18. Is it now worth reviewing questions 13 to 17 for your 'second choice' individual?

19. Do you expect your own immediate staff to adopt the same planned approach to development? Are they quite clear about what you expect? Are you sure?

- What periodic checks do you make to ensure that what you want to happen does indeed happen?
- Should such checks be stepped up?
- How often do you meet with your immediate staff to discuss succession planning? Is that often enough?

20. Are you genuinely in a position to commit to paper your plans for people's movements in your area? Over the next year? The following year? A longer period? If you cannot, then it is more likely that your area will plan you rather than the reverse?

Remember:

If your succession planning is effective you are much less likely to be caught with your nether garments around your ankles, or even suffer the ignominy of having them nailed to the organizational mast! Of course you will manage if a key person leaves, but will you manage well?

34   Suggestions schemes

The staff of an organization represent a fruitful source of new ideas for improving corporate effectiveness which can remain largely untapped. A well publicized suggestions scheme which is seen to be fair in its awards can provide a powerful stimulus in the search for higher productivity.

1. Does your organization operate a suggestions scheme?

    − If not, when was the possibility last considered?
    − What were the reasons, specifically, for rejecting such a scheme?
    − Should these reasons be re-examined now in the light of current circumstances?

2. If your organization does operate a suggestions scheme, what are its objectives? Is everyone aware of what these objectives are? If not, what should be done? By whom?

3. Is the scheme designed to allow all employees to participate? If not, why? Who is excluded? Should they be excluded? Should the objectives be reconsidered?

4. Are the scales of awards realistic?

    − When were they last reviewed?
    − Do they really motivate employees? How do you know?
    − Have incentives other than cash been considered (e.g. additional leave days, etc.)?

5. Is the scheme well publicized?

    − Is it explained during induction?
    − Are explanatory leaflets readily available?
    − Are supervision/management fully briefed?
    − Is publicity given to recent awards?

    If not, what action should be taken? By whom? When?

6. Have you ever considered the advisability of conducting an attitude survey to establish reactions to the schemes? If so, what was the result?

7. Against what criteria is the worth of suggestions assessed? Are the following possible areas of improvement included in the assessment?

   - Quality?
   - Human resource utilization?
   - Accident prevention?
   - Working conditions?
   - Material usage?
   - Working methods?
   - Tools and machinery usage?
   - Communications?
   - Effectiveness of training (doing the right things)?
   - Operating costs?
   - Efficiency of training (doing things right)?
   - Supplier-user interface?

   What other areas of possible improvement could, and should, be introduced in the future?

8. Do all concerned understand the basis on which awards are made? Are you absolutely sure?

   - Is the position on patent rights absolutely clear?
   - Is there an appeals procedure? Does it work?

9. What is the average time lag between a suggestion being put forward and a final decision on its worth being made?

   - Is that too long?
   - Should the introduction of interim awards be considered?
   - Are the orginators of suggestions kept fully in the picture?
   - Are you sure?

10. Who is responsible for assessing the worth of individual suggestions? Are these the right people?

11. Is there a review committee? If not, why? If so, when was the last time its constitution was checked? By whom? With what result?

12. Is it time new blood was brought into the committee? Could membership be used as a personal development exercise for selected staff?

13. How often does the committee meet? Are the meetings held:

    - Regularly at specified intervals?
    - When there are sufficient suggestions to consider?

    Should the timing be reviewed?

14.   Is there any other basis on which your organization's suggestions scheme might be improved? If so, why are you delaying?

35 Training and development strategy

As with any form of organizational decision-making, strategic considerations ('what needs to be done?') must precede tactical issues ('how should it be achieved?') Unless training and development activities accurately reflect corporate strategy they can never be successful. Certainly training and development must be efficient (doing things right) although such efficiency must be squarely matched by effectiveness (doing the right thing).

Your organization

1. Why does your organization exist? What is its mission? Is a statement of this mission available in written form? To whom? Are those the right people? Are you sure?

2. What are your organization's aims and objectives?

   - Have those aims and objectives also been committed to paper? Clearly? Unambiguously?
   - If not, are you sure your initial response is accurate?
   - If so, is such a written statment available to *all* employees of the organization?
   - What would be the answers of your colleagues and other employees to these questions?

3. Will your organization's mission change in the foreseeable future?

   - If so, in what possible ways? Will these changes require modification of the mission statement?
   - Could your organization's whole *raison d'etre* change? How? In what direction might it move?

4. Within which business sector(s) does your organization currently operate?

   - What is the current business/product portfolio?

- What resources does this portfolio demand?
  - To what extent may the portfolio change in, say, the next five years? A longer period?
    - What are the resource requirement implications of your answer? Can you identify the probable 'resource gap'?

5. What are the current strategic strengths of your organization?

    - What opportunities for growth/change/modification are arising now from these strengths within the organization?
    - What opportunities could arise in the future?

6. What are the strategic weaknesses of your organization, if any?

    - What threats do these weaknesses represent now?
    - What threats could they represent in the future?

7. What other external factors may particularly affect your organization in the future? How? To what extent?

Training and development implications

8. Having identified what your organization is, and what it has (markets, resources, etc.), and compared the result with what the organization could become in the future, what are the broad implications for the training and development function? Now? In the future?

9. Why does the training and development function exist in your organization? What is its contribution to the achievement of the corporate mission? In what principal ways does it support this mission?

10. What are the current aims and objectives of the training and development function?

    - Have these aims and objectives been committed to paper? Coherently? Are you sure?
      - Who decided what these aims and objectives should be? In consultation with who else?
      - What time-scales do they cover?
      - How often are they reviewed? Is that often enough in a rapidly-changing environment?
      - Who is informed of the aims and objectives? How are they informed?
      - Are *all* key personnel informed?
    - What are the implications of your answers to these questions? What could/should you be doing to enhance the impact of training and development activities on corporate performance?

174

11. What is the current training and development portfolio (See Figure 35.1)?

– How closely does this portfolio reflect the aims and objectives identified in response to question 10?
– Is the portfolio really suitable for its present market? How do you know?
– Is the portfolio too large? Or too small? By what criteria?
– In what direction is the portfolio likely to move over, say, the next five years? In response to which particular forces?

Express as percentage of total training and development activity:

	Initial	Booster	Retraining
Apprentice			
Craft			
Operator			
Technician			
Supervisory			
Management			
Specialist			
Other			

Figure 35.1   Current training and development portfolio

12. What are the strategic strengths of the training and development function in your organization? How does your answer compare with your response to question 3? What action, if any is indicated?

– What opportunities for growth/change/modification are arising now from these strengths? What opportunities could arise in the future?
– Just how far is line management supportive of training and development initiatives in your organization? To what extent is it actively involved?
   • Is direct training and development responsibility accepted as an integral part of every management post in your organization?
   • If so, how can such acceptance be harnessed more effectively than at present?
   • If not, what should be done to modify current perceptions? What could be done over the next six months? The next year? What will be done?

13. What, if any, are the current strategic weaknesses within the training and development function?

– What threats do these weaknesses represent now? What threats

could they represent in the future?
— Where is the primary training and development effort currently focused?
  ● How was this focus decided? When? By whom?
  ● Was it genuinely decided? Or is the focus blurred? To what extent?
— Is this the most effective focus when considered against current organizational needs? Future needs?
  ● What resources are utilized now to support this effort?
  ● What is the current resource allocation?
  ● What resource *reallocation* may be necessary to define the focus more effectively?

14. Reviewing your answers to these questions about training and development in relation to where your organization is now and where it is going in the foreseeable future, is the function responding to opportunities from a position of strength? Or does a critical weakness lie in its purely reactive response to current (and future) needs?

15. Is the training and development function effective in its efforts? Is it aware of opportunities? Is it truly active? Or does it tend to be excluded from, and therefore remain unaware of, strategic business discussions?

16. Which description, shown in Figure 35.2, appears to be most accurate in relation to the training and development function in your organization?

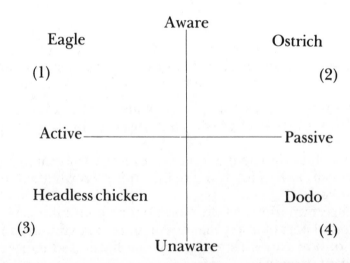

Aware

Eagle   Ostrich

(1)   (2)

Active————————————Passive

Headless chicken   Dodo

(3)   (4)

Unaware

Eagle
Fully aware of what it is doing. Sharp-eyed for opportunities. A high flier, operating from a position of strength.

Headless chicken
Mistakes motion for direction *and* activity for action. Going absolutely nowhere, but doesn't know it.

Ostrich
Only aware of what is happening up to a point. Then sticks its head in the sand to hide from events: a vulnerable stance which tends to invite the obvious response.

Dodo
Extinct now because in the past it was both passive and unaware. Now only referred to in books.

Figure 35.2   Effectiveness of the training and development function

17. Having located training and development in the appropriate quadrant, what action is suggested by your response?

  – What are the strategic choices open to you now?
  – What alternative strategies should be considered? Can you locate these alternatives in Figure 35.3?

Choices	Training and development focus now	Alternative training and development focus
Short term (up to 1 year) 1 2 3 4 5		
Medium term (1–2 years) 1 2 3 4 5		
Longer term (2+years) 1 2 3 4 5		

Figure 35.3 Strategic choices

18. Are you now in a position to evaluate these choices? Against what criteria?

  – Degree of risk?
  – Degree of effort involved?
  – Political impact?
  – Cost against budget?
  – Or what?

19. Can you rank the choices in order of importance? And weight them (say in percentage terms)?

20. What action is indicated by your analysis? Is it time now for your decisions? Can you *choose*?

21. What resources are necessary to implement your choices?
    - Are they available?
    - If not, can they be made available? How? How soon?

22. How should these resources be allocated. To what extent should they be reallocated?

23. How will you ensure that the choices you have implemented are evaluated periodically? What should the assessment period be? Ideally? Practically? Who should be involved? Who should be informed of the outcomes?

24. What do you intend to do *now* to improve the situation?